Port

Simon Stephens' play *Bring Me Sunshine* was staged at the Assembly Rooms at the 1997 Edinburgh Fringe Festival, transferring to the Riverside Studios in London the same year (revived in 2000 at the Manchester Royal Exchange). His next play, *Bluebird*, was produced by the Royal Court in London in 1998. Simon Stephens was writer-in-residence at the Royal Exchange Theatre in 1999 and in 2000 he was the Arts Council Resident Dramatist at the Royal Court. His next play, *Herons* (Royal Court 2001), was nominated for the Olivier Award for Most Promising Playwright. His radio play *Five Letters Home to Elizabeth* was broadcast on Radio 4 in 2001 and *Digging* will be on Radio 4 in 2003. *Port* was awarded the Pearson Award for Best New Play in 2001/2 and *One Minute* will be produced by the Actors Touring Company in June 2003.

Published by Methuen Drama

1 3 5 7 9 10 8 6 4 2

First published in 2002 by
Methuen Publishing Limited

ISBN 0 413 77311 6

Typeset by SX Composing DTP, Rayleigh, Essex
Printed and bound in Great Britain by
Cox & Wyman Ltd, Reading, Berkshire

Caution

Acknowledgment

The quotation on page iv is from *Cathedral*
by Raymond Carver. Reprinted by permission
of the Random House Group Limited.

Port

Simon Stephens

Methuen Drama

Nicky. Betty. Hazel. Christine. Sharon. Jane. Ta.

This play, like everything, is for Poll.

'Suppose, just suppose, nothing had ever happened.
Suppose this was for the first time. It doesn't hurt to
suppose. Say none of the other had happened. You know
what I mean? Then what? I said.'

Raymond Carver, *Chef's House*

Characters

Racheal Keats, *11–24*
Billy Keats, *6–10/19*
Danny Miller, *15/24*
Christine Keats, *29* }
Anne Dickinson, *74* }
Jonathan Keats, *34* }
Kevin Brake, 28 }
Lucy Moore, *15*
Chris Bennett, *15*
Ronald Abbey, *50* }
Jake Moran, *48* }
Man in Home, *73* }

The characters that are bracketed together should be played by the same actor. Although distinct there are fundamental shared resonances in their relationships with Racheal Keats.

This play takes place in a variety of locations in and around Stockport, Greater Manchester between 1988 and 2002.

The set should remain spare and non-naturalistic throughout. The locations should be evoked by space, detail and lighting rather than replicated.

The character of Racheal Keats must remain on stage throughout the play. In between scenes we should be able to observe the adoption of nuances of physicality, aspect and dress that the actor employs in order to dramatise her increasing maturity.

An interval may fall after Scene Five.

A note on punctuation:
    – denotes interruption or a sudden halt
    ... denotes a trailing off

Port premiered at the Royal Exchange Theatre, Manchester on 12th November 2002. The cast was as follows:

Racheal Keats	Emma Lowndes
Billy Keats	Andrew Sheridan
Danny Miller	William Ash
Christine Keats/Anne Dickinson	Siobhan Finneran
Jonathan Keats/Kevin Brake	Nicholas Siddi
Ronald Abbey/Jake Moran	Fred Ridgeway
Chris Bennet	Colin Parry
Lucy Moore	Rachel Brogan

Directed by Marianne Elliott
Designed by Rae Smith
Lighting Designed by John Buswell
Sound Designed by Ian Dickinson

The play was written while the writer was on a Pearson Residency at the Royal Exchange Theatre; he would like to acknowledge the support of Pearson Television. He would also like to acknowledge the support of all the staff at the Royal Exchange Theatre, especially Sarah Frankcom; the staff and members of the YWP at the Royal Court Theatre, London and the ever mighty Mel Kenyon.

This text was complete and accurate before the start of rehearsals. It does not include any changes that may have occurred throughout the rehearsal period.

Scene One

1988. A parked Vauxhall Cavalier in the car park of the flats on Lancashire Hill in Stockport. We should see the exposed interior of the car towards one edge of the stage. A real Vauxhall Cavalier should be used. The top of the car should be sawn off.

Isolating light on the car.

Racheal Keats, *eleven years old, sits in the passenger seat eating a bar of Dairy Milk.* **Billy Keats**, *six years old, sits slumped on the back seat. She wears a blue Adidas tracksuit top over her school uniform. He wears a huge battered Kappa coat over his.* **Christine Keats**, *their mother, twenty-nine years old, sits in the driver's seat.*

It is midnight.

Christine Keats *stares fixedly up at the fifth-floor flat where she lives with her children. Her husband, their father,* **Jonathan**, *is in there.*

The children are lively, excited. Throughout the scene the children's activity should be uninhibited, exploratory.

Christine *is desperately trying to ignore her children. This is her only means of tolerating their excitement.*

Billy *kicks the back of* **Racheal**'s *seat repeatedly. We should see his kicking. Maybe he sits raised up on the back seat. Maybe he even stands.*

Racheal   Billy.

He continues.

Billy, stop it.

He doesn't.

Billy, stop kicking me. God!

Billy   What?

Racheal   Mum. Tell him.

Billy   I'm not doing anything.

Racheal   Mum, will you tell him? He keeps kicking the back of my chair.

Billy   I don't. It's her.

Christine (*without turning*)   Billy, stop it. Now.

Billy   God. I'm not doing anything. Always sticking up for her. She's always lying about me. Always saying I'm doing stuff when I'm never. 'S so not fair.

Christine (*with a glare*)   Billy, one more word. I'm warning yer.

Billy *slumps back in his chair. Gives her the finger behind her back.*

Pause.

Billy *kneels up on the back seat and looks out of the side and back windows of the car.*

Billy   Mum.

What?

Billy   Mum.

Christine   What?

Billy   Mum.

Christine   What, Billy, for fuck's sake?

Billy   When are we going to Disney World Florida?

Christine   Oh, Jesus fucking Christ, Billy, would you shut your gob for one second, would yer? For fuck's sake.

He slumps back on the car seat. Huffs. Glares daggers into her back. Brief time.

Racheal   Mum. You know what Billy told me? You know what he told me? He told me. He goes. You know that path up our school, Mum?

Billy (*sitting up, urgent*)   I never.

He pushes his head between the front two seats.

Racheal (*grinning*)   He goes, if you walk off that path. If you go off the side of it and hop up and down three times –

Billy (*trying to thump her*)   I never. Liar.

Racheal (*chuckling, ignoring the thumps*)   You did, Billy. Stop lying. He goes, if you do that, he goes, you go to a magic place.

Billy (*slumping back, pissed off*)   I never said that.

Racheal (*with a big bite of chocolate*)   He's a dickhead.

Billy   I hate you.

Racheal   Int he, Mum? Int he a dickhead?

Billy   Shut it.

Racheal   No.

Billy   I'm gonna kill you.

Racheal (*with delighted mock horror*)   Mum. You hear that? You hear what he says? Mum heard that! You're going to go to Borstal now.

Billy   Fuck off.

Christine   Billy, shut it.

Christine *turns in her seat and smacks* **Billy** *in the face.* **Billy** *sits back in his chair. Holds his head down. Tries not to sob.* **Christine** *glares back at the window.* **Racheal** *sits still.*

Racheal   He should be asleep. Shouldn't he? Mum? Shouldn't he be asleep? Tell him, Mum. Tell him to go to sleep. He'll be knackered tomorrow. Falling asleep on his desk and that. Dribbling on his books. Proper gypsy. Should see him. I've seen him in assembly. Snoring. He's a right tramp.

Billy (*through his teeth*)   Am not.

Racheal   I saw Mrs Greenside with him. She was dead mad. Should have seen her. She gets him. Right in front of everyone. In her class and that. In juniors. And she gets him to the front of the class and she pulls his pants down and smacks his bum. Bare and everything. He was crying. Weren't yer?

Billy (*after a pause*)   No.

Racheal (*finishing the chocolate*)   You were, Billy. I saw you.

Billy   I weren't, right?

Christine (*still staring up at window*)   Go to sleep, Billy.

Pause. **Billy** *lies down in back seat.*

Billy   Can't.

Christine   You're not trying. Close yer eyes.

Some time. **Billy** *is still.*

Racheal (*quietly*)   Mum.

Christine   What?

Racheal   Why's our Billy always getting run over?

Christine   I don't know.

Racheal   Three times now, int it? Normal people don't get run over three times. Do they, Mum?

Christine   I don't know.

Racheal   I hate Mrs Greenside. She's got really bony wrists.

Silence.

He's going to sleep now. (*Singing, gently.*) 'Rock-a-bye baby on the tree top. When the wind the wind blows the cradle will rock –'

Christine   Shut it, Rachel. Fucking going on.

Racheal   I were only singing.

Christine   Well, don't.

Racheal   I was trying to get him to sleep.

Christine   Well, leave him.

Pause.

Racheal (*with a big shrug*)   Mum.

Christine   What?

Racheal   You remember when I got my hand caught int' mangle?

Christine   You what?

Racheal   Did that hurt?

Christine   What?

Racheal   Did it hurt when I got my hand caught int' mangle and that?

Christine   I don't know, do I? It were your hand.

Racheal   I don't remember it. Probably blanked it out of my memory, an't I? What's the first thing you can remember?

Christine (*still watching window*)   I don't know.

Racheal   You know what first thing I can remember is?

Christine   No.

Racheal   I remember finding that dead sparrow. In our yard. You remember that? When I did that. Picked it up. Put it in a paper tissue. You remember? Bring it to you? All the bones and that. Dead tiny. You went crackers.

No response. Some time.

She thinks aloud, counting aloud, proving something that she learned at school to her mum.

Next year it'll be 1989. And then it'll be two years and that'll be the new decade and that'll be the nineties and then it'll be ten years and that'll be the new century. We did that at school.

No response. **Christine** *watches the window. Some time.*

I'll be twenty-three. God!

No response. Some time.

You know summit?

Christine (*still at window, but conceding gently*)   What?

Racheal   Sometimes, when you fart, it smells quite nice. You ever notice that? Yer own farts and that.

Christine (*turns to her*)   Racheal!

Racheal   It's true.

Christine   You're disgusting.

Racheal   You know summit else I think?

Christine   What?

Racheal   I think this is nice.

Beat. **Christine** *looks at her. Then back at the window.*

Christine   It's not.

Racheal   I think it is. I think it's all right. I do. I like it. You know what it's like? You remember when I was little. In the morning sometimes. You used to get us. Put us in your bed. To keep you warm. Always said I was like your hot-water bottle. Didn't you? You remember that? Mum? Do you? It's like that, I reckon.

Christine *looks at her briefly. Lights a cigarette and then looks back up at the window.* **Racheal** *opens another bar of Dairy Milk.*

Racheal   Shouldn't smoke. Not with our Billy asleep and that. Wind window down.

Christine   It's freezing.

Beat.

Racheal   You know when I grow up?

Christine   Yeah.

Racheal   You know who I want to be like?

Christine   Who?

Racheal   Leanne's mum.

Christine (*turning to her*)   You what?!?

Racheal   I think she's beautiful, I do.

Christine   You do not.

Racheal   I do. I think she's dead glamorous and everything.

Christine   Racheal, she's a fucking whore.

Racheal   So! That's what I want to be then!

Christine   Racheal!

Racheal   I do! I think she's beautiful. You should dress like her, Mum. You should. All the make-up and that.

Christine (*away again*)   You don't know what you're talking about.

Pause. **Racheal** *scans the windows of the car. Kneels up in her passenger seat to look around her. Perhaps sits on the top of the passenger door.*

Racheal   I like it here.

Christine   Do you?

Racheal   I like the park. Me and Leanne go up park sometimes. Did you know that?

Christine   No.

Racheal   We do.

Christine   You should watch it.

Racheal   Come and look for men.

Christine   For what?

Racheal   Men come up park sometimes. Get their willies out. We look for 'em. Scream at 'em. Peg it. It's dead funny.

Christine *laughs despite herself.* **Racheal** *puffs up with pride.*

Christine   You wanna watch that. All the perverts and that. Racheal, honestly.

Racheal   Ronald Abbey. He's a pervert. (*Beat.*) Can see the river from here. It's good down there. Stinks. But there's good stuff.

Christine   What sort of stuff?

Racheal   Just stuff that people leave. I like the water.

Christine (*serious*)   Racheal, it's filthy.

Racheal   I still like it.

Christine (*firmly*)   You better not go swimming in it.

Racheal   You what?

Christine   That water's filthy. You better not go swimming in it.

Racheal   Course not. I'm not thick, am I? Look, Mum. Can see clock tower in Merseyway. It's massive. It's a skyscraper that is, int it? Mum?

Christine   Is it fuck a skyscraper.

Racheal   I think it is. (*Long silence. She yawns. Looks up to her mother.*) Smells of tarmac.

Christine   What does?

Racheal   Here. In summer.

Christine   I don't know what you're going on about half the time.

Pause. **Racheal** *kneels up to look over into the back seat.*

Racheal   Billy's asleep.

Christine   Good.

Racheal   He looks right peaceful. He looks dead little when he's asleep doesn't he?

Christine   Who?

Racheal   Billy. I wish he'd stop getting, you know, stop getting run over. He keeps going on about Disney World Florida and that.

Christine   I know.

Racheal   You gonna take him?

Christine   I don't know.

Racheal   Mum.

Christine   Racheal.

Racheal   Why's he done this?

Christine   What?

Racheal   Dad. Why's he done this?

Christine   I don't know, love.

Racheal   It's mental. As if you do this! As if you do though!

Christine   Racheal.

Racheal *turns back, sits up on her heels.*

Racheal   It is though, int it? Mental and that. You reckon he's in there?

Christine   Course he is.

Racheal   Lights off. Door locked. Sitting in there?

Christine   I could hear him.

Racheal   I hate it when he goes like this.

Christine   So do I.

Racheal   Why does he go like this, Mum? Mum? Why does he? Why does he go like dead mental and that?

Christine   I don't know.

Racheal   You're his wife.

Christine   So?

Racheal   You must know.

Christine   Would you shut up?

Racheal   You must though, mustn't you? There must be a reason.

Christine   Rachel, I'll fucking thump yer.

Racheal   You wouldn't.

Christine   You wanna try me?

Beat.

Racheal   I'm frightened of him.

Christine   You are not.

Racheal   I am. He's weird, he is.

Christine   He's your dad. He's not weird.

Racheal   Way he looks at us sometimes.

Christine   He's never weird.

Racheal   I think he hates us.

Christine   Don't be daft.

Racheal   Must though. Mustn't he? Big fat fucking bastard.

Silence.

This doesn't happen to most people, you know. Most normal people.

Christine   How do you know?

Racheal   It doesn't.

Pause. **Racheal** *stares at her mother who has taken to staring out of her side window.*

Racheal   Mum.

Christine   Racheal.

Racheal   What you thinking? Mum? Mum, what are you thinking? Tell us.

Christine   Has he put a light on?

Racheal   You gonna tell us or what.

Christine   Has he, Rache? Is that our flat?

Racheal   I don't know. I can't tell.

They crane their necks to look. And then settle back. **Christine** *lights another cigarette.*

Christine   You shouldn't say that he's weird. All right?

Racheal   Why shouldn't I? He is. He shouldn't lock us out of the flat, should he? Dickhead.

Christine   Racheal. Don't.

Racheal (*a little upset*)   Do you like him?

Christine   Course I do.

Racheal   Do you really?

Christine   You should go to sleep.

Pause. **Racheal** *settles down. Nestles her head against her seat belt.*

Racheal (*looking into wing mirror*)   You know Sarah Briard?

Christine   Who?

Racheal (*back to* **Christine**)   Sarah Briard. Out of our class.

Christine   No.

Racheal   She's dead.

Christine   You what?

Racheal   She got smacked by a car. She was ten. Imagine that. Imagine being ten and you're dead. That's dead sad that is, int it? All the stuff she wanted to do, all that stuff. She's never ever going to do that now. Not none of it. Wanted to play for Man U and everything. Fucking thick cow. As if you play for Man U and you're a girl. I never liked her. She was fat.

Christine   Racheal.

Racheal   Are you going to tell me what you were thinking?

Christine   What?

Racheal   Are you?

Christine   No.

Racheal   You know what I think you were thinking.

Christine   Racheal, for fuck's sake.

Racheal   I think you were thinking all about Dad and all about this and about how mental it is and about us and about how you want to kill him and about how much you love him, and about whether you're going to leave him and about whether you're going to leave us and about how old Billy is and about how old I am and about whether you're going to go and I think that you think that you're going to. That's what I think. Am I right?

Christine   No.

Racheal   What were you thinking then?

Christine   I'm not going to tell you.

Racheal   Liar. I can always tell when you're lying.

Billy *cries out, half asleep. He remains lying down.*

Billy   I want to go in that car. I want to go in that car. Mum. I want to go in that car.

Christine   Billy? Billy? Billy, love? You're dreaming!

Billy   What?

Christine   You were having a dream.

Billy   What?

Christine   You were dreaming. Started crying out. Go back to sleep.

Billy (*sitting up, his head between the two front seats*)   Where are we?

Christine   We're in the car, love. Outside. It's all right. Go back to sleep, sweetheart.

He settles. They wait until he is.

Racheal (*quietly*)   Funny bugger. 'I want to go in that car!' What car? Bloody beamer, is it? Kip in a Merc, is it?

Christine   You should go to sleep and all.

Racheal   It's mad this, int it?

Christine   What?

Racheal   This. It's a bit mad, I think. Don't you reckon?

Christine   It is a little.

Racheal   You should tell Grandad. Imagine this and you told Grandad. He'd go barmy. He'd smash Dad's head in, I reckon. Don't you reckon, Mum? Don't you think you should tell him?

Christine   I don't think so, love, no.

Racheal   I like Grandad. He's a right mad bastard. (*Beat.*) Nana's a bit weird but Grandad's all right. Funny pipe-cleaners and that. Mad Joe 90 goggles. Mum. (*Beat.*) Are you thinking of going? Mum?

Christine   No.

Racheal   I wouldn't blame you. Dad's a knobhead.

Christine   Racheal.

Racheal   You could take us with you.

Christine   You what?

Racheal   You could. You could take us with you. We could go now. We could just leave. Wouldn't need no bags or nothing. Nothing like that. Just start driving. Go to Grandad's and not come back. Go to country. Go to Disney World Florida. Couldn't we though, Mum? I reckon that'd be a top idea.

Christine   Racheal.

Racheal   I reckon that'd be well smart. Me and you and Billy in Dad's car. Pissing off with no bags or nothing. Going to Disneyland Florida. Don't you reckon that'd be sound? It would though, Mum, wouldn't it?

Christine   Racheal.

Racheal   What?

Christine (*quietly, menacing*)   Just, fucking shut it, would ya?

Racheal   What?

Christine (*still menacing*)   We're not going to Disney World Florida. We're not going to countryside. We're not going anywhere. Jesus. Do you think? Do you really think that if I wanted to bugger off from here then I'd take you wirr us? I'm not daft, am I? Am I daft? No. No I'm not. Bloody dead weight, you two. Int you? Pair of yous. I'd piss off on me tod. Leave you two to fuckhead.

Racheal   Mum, don't.

Christine   We're not going. All right? We're staying put. You hear me? Do you?

Racheal   Yeah.

Pause. **Racheal** *screws up her chocolate wrapper. Stares at it. Then looks to her mum.* **Christine** *stares up at the window.*

Lights dim. In the dimness **Christine** *exits.* **Racheal** *removes her tracksuit top.* **Billy** *pulls up the zip of his coat and lifts the hood above his head. Perhaps the car remains on stage throughout.*

Scene Two

1990. The cafe of Stepping Hill Hospital, Stockport.
We see a white plastic wipe-clean table with yellow plastic trim. Four plastic moulded seats attached to the table. The whole stage is lit very brightly. An antiseptic white light. There is a large bottle fridge full of Fanta Orange.
It is nine o'clock at night. **Billy Keats**, *aged eight, sits on one side of the table.* **Racheal Keats**, *aged thirteen, sits on the other.*
They are both doing their homework. **Billy** *holds his pen in his fist. He is unsettled. He unzips and zips up his coat repeatedly. After a short while he pulls his hood down. Sits grinning at* **Racheal**.
Racheal *sits up straighter. She throws occasional glances at her brother. As though these glances will rein in his attention to his homework. They won't.*
They continue with their work for a few seconds. **Racheal** *looks up at him.*

Racheal   What is it?

Billy   What?

Racheal   Yer homework.

Billy (*looking at the Fanta fridge*)   Maths.

Racheal   Yer want any help?

Billy   No. It's easy. It's adding up. It's stupid.

Racheal   If you get stuck. Just ask us.

She looks down. Continues with her work.

Mine's geography. My homework. (*Beat. Looking to him.*) Continental drift. Did you know that you're moving?

Billy (*looking back to her*)   Yer what?

Racheal   Right now. You're moving. Stockport's moving. England's moving. Getting closer and closer to America. Gonna smash up into it. Big fucking pile-up. Did yer know that? I bet yer never, did ya?

Billy   When?

Racheal   Not for ages. Thousands and thousands and thousands and thousands of years. Yer'll be dead. Before it happens.

Billy   Won't.

Racheal   Yer will. Like Grandad.

Billy   I'm gonna live for ever me.

Racheal   Yer not.

Billy   Grandad's never dead.

Racheal   Will be soon. Probably is already. Probably in there. Dead. Hope he is.

Pause. **Billy** *rests his head on the table. On his book. Writes with his fist.*

Lift yer head off the table.

Billy   Am thinking.

Racheal   Can't think with yer head on the table. Yer'll fall asleep.

Billy   Shut up. Yer not me mum.

Pause.

Racheal   Don't write like that. Yer not an idiot. Don't hold yer pen like that. Hold it properly.

Billy *looks long and hard at* **Racheal**. *Then looks around the room. Back at the fridge again.*

Billy (*enthralled*)   Look. They got Fanta Orange. In the fridge. Get us some.

Racheal   I've not got any money. Dad never gave us any money.

Billy *stands. Takes his coat off and drops it on the floor by the table.*

Billy   Am gonna nick some. Yer want some? I'll nick it. They won't do out.

Racheal   Billy, sit down.

Billy (*goes to leave the table*)   They won't do nothing. They're fucking lazy bastards. Watch 'em.

Racheal   Billy, I'm warning you. Sit down.

He slumps back down in his chair.

Thieving little gypsy.

Billy (*head in hands now*)   He should have given us some money. I'm really thirsty.

Racheal   Well, he never. He'll be back soon. Just wait.

Billy   Mum'd have give us some money. She'd have let us nick a bottle anyways. (*Pause, looks at her. Brightly, inquisitive.*) Rache. What yer reckon it's like? Being dead?

Racheal   Better than what's happening to him.

Billy *stands. Leaves the table. Begins to explore the whole space. She tries to persuade him to come back to the table with the words that she says.*

Billy   Why?

Racheal   Yer see him?

Billy   No.

Racheal   Should have seen him. Flapping around and that. Screaming.

Billy   Was he?

Racheal   I saw him last week. He were like a fish. It was mental. You know what I'm going to do?

Billy   What?

Racheal   I'm going to go in there. And kill him. Put him out of his misery. Stop him flapping around and that.

Billy   Yer what?

Racheal   I'm going to. I've decided.

Billy   Yer fucking not.

Racheal   I am. There must be summit in here, eh? Be good, wouldn't it? Imagine it, Billy. Gagging for breath he'd be. Like a mongoloid.

Billy   Yer wouldn't.

Racheal   I fucking would.

Billy   You're nuts, you are.

Racheal   It'd be mental.

Billy   You're crackers. I think you're on drugs.

Racheal   Yer what?

Billy   I think you are. I'm gonna tell our dad. You take drugs. You smoke drugs. You smoke blow.

Racheal   I don't.

Billy   I bet yer do. I bet yer on it right now. Stoned off yer fucking head.

Racheal   Billy. Shut up or I'll fucking thump yer.

Billy   So? I'd thump yer back. Where's our mum?

Racheal   I don't know.

Billy   Yer must do. It's her dad. She should be here by now. And Nana. Where's she?

She stares at him for a while. And then looks away.

Racheal   Yer know summit?

Billy   What?

Racheal When Grandad gets better. When he comes out. Am gonna go and live wiv 'em.

Billy (*returning to the table*) Yer never.

Racheal I am. Dad said. You're not coming with us. Just me and Nana and Grandad. It'll be fucking great.

Billy Fuck off.

Racheal *chuckles briefly*.

Racheal Did you see that kid in the lift?

Billy What?

Racheal When we got in the lift to come down? Did yer see the kid getting out of the lift?

Billy No. What about him?

Racheal It were horrible. He was all crippled up. All bandaged up. Every part of him. Looked like a mummy. He was tiny and all.

Billy *giggles. Sits sideways on to the table, facing the fridge.*

Racheal It's not funny, Billy.

Billy Yeah, it is.

Racheal It's not, Billy. It's horrible. This place is all fucking horrible.

Billy I like it. I think it's all right. They've got Fanta Orange. Chocolate. It's good.

Ronald Abbey *enters. A man of indistinguishable weight. Fifty years old. Milk-bottle spectacles. Thinning hair. He speaks with a certain amount of saliva rattling around his teeth, smiles inappropriately nearly all the time and blinks a lot. He never, ever looks at the people he addresses. His evasion becoming more pronounced as the conversation becomes more personal. The children think he is, by turns, disgusting and hilarious. For a short time he hugs the side of the stage.*

Ronald   Hello, Billy. Racheal. Your dad said you were down here.

Billy   Arright, Ronald?

Racheal   Ronald.

Ronald   How are the two of you?

Billy   Arright, thank you.

Racheal   You been to see Grandad?

Billy *starts giggling again.*

Ronald   Yes. Yes I have.

Racheal   How is he?

Ronald   He was sleeping.

Billy *does fake snoring. And then continues to giggle.*

Racheal   Billy. Shut it.

Ronald   I wanted to say. I'm very sorry. About your grandad. And everything. I like him very much. He's a good person.

Racheal   It's all right, Ronald. He's going to get better soon.

Ronald   I do hope so.

Racheal   He will.

Ronald (*moving closer to their table, almost circling it*)   Are you bearing up? The two of you? Is everything OK?

Racheal   Yes. We're fine thank you very much. Billy, shut it.

Ronald   And your dad, is he all right?

Racheal   I think he's fine, yes.

Ronald   And have you heard anything from your mum?

Racheal   No we've not.

Ronald   I see. How long has that been now?

Racheal   Fourteen months.

Ronald   I see.

Racheal   On Tuesday.

Ronald   Good. Right. Well. If there's anything I can do for you. Anything at all. You know where I am.

Billy *bursts out laughing.* **Racheal** *stands, pissed off with* **Billy,** *backs away from* **Ronald.** **Billy** *remains seated between the two of them.*

Racheal   Billy. For fuck's sake.

Ronald   No, no. Racheal. That's all right. Is there something the matter, Billy?

Billy   No.

Ronald   Is there something very funny happening?

Billy   I know where you are.

Ronald   I'm sorry?

Billy   You said, 'You know where I am.' And I do. I know where you are. All the time. Up Lancy Hill.

Ronald *(closer)*   I'm sorry?

Billy *(rocking on his chair, drumming on his legs)*   Int he? She's seen yer. She tells us. Yer up there all the time. Get yer knob out and everything, don't yer?

Ronald   Maybe I should go.

Billy   Don't he? You said.

Ronald   Did she?

Racheal   Billy. You're dead.

Billy   Why? It's true.

Ronald *(closer still)*   Did she say that, did she?

Billy   Yeah. Get yer dick out for the little girls and that.

Racheal   I swear.

Billy   Can I see it, Ronald? Will yer gerrit out for us now? Will yer?

Ronald (*standing quite still, grinning*)   Well. Racheal.

Racheal   Ronald. I never.

Ronald (*still grinning, looking away from her, quietly*)   You little whore.

Racheal   Ronald!

Ronald   You little tart.

Racheal   Yer what?

Ronald   With your brother, Racheal. Surely not even you could go that far.

Racheal   What did you say?

Ronald   You heard me.

Racheal   I don't believe that.

Ronald   You heard me.

Moves to leave. **Jonathan Keats** *enters. Thirty-four years old. A sinewy man. Tattooed. Shaven-headed. He almost never registers any outward sign of emotional engagement. He is drinking coffee from a paper cup. He has a presence which registers immediately, not only with the children but also with* **Ronald**, *regardless of where they are looking. There is a stillness about him that is impressive.*

Jonathan   Arright, Ronald.

Racheal   Dad. You should have heard what he just said. I swear.

Ronald   Hello, Jonathan. Everything all right?

Jonathan   Everything's fine, mate. Yeah. Not bad.

Racheal   Honestly, Dad. Billy. Shouldn't he?

Jonathan (*without really registering*)   What?

Racheal   Hear what Ronald just said.

Jonathan   Why?

Racheal   It was barmy.

Ronald   I should be going.

Jonathan   Right. OK. Thank you for coming.

Ronald   No. Not at all. I was saying to Racheal and Billy. I like Gordon. He's a good man.

Racheal   I'm going to tell him. Ronald. After you've gone.

Jonathan   Tell him what? Tell who? What's going on?

Ronald   I must go. There's a bus. I'll see you soon I hope, Jonathan.

Jonathan   Yes. Right. I hope so too, Ronald. I'll see you later.

Ronald   G'bye, Racheal. Billy.

Billy   Tarrah.

Racheal (*laughing*)   Yeah. See yer, Ronald.

He exits opposite **Racheal**. **Billy** *and* **Racheal** *laughing bewildered as he leaves.*

I swear.

Jonathan   What's going on?

Racheal   You should have heard what he was saying. He's a psycho that one, Dad. I'm telling yer.

Jonathan   What did he say?

Racheal (*going to collect her homework up*)   Nothing. It don't matter.

Jonathan   Why? What was it?

Racheal   It was nothing. I'll tell yer later.

Jonathan   Right.

He moves towards the table. Sits down. Looks straight ahead for a few seconds before he speaks. Drinks from his cup.

Racheal. Billy. Yer grandad's died.

Billy *bursts out laughing again.*

Jonathan   Just now. In his sleep and that.

Racheal (*crushed*)   He never.

Jonathan   He has, love. I'm sorry.

Billy's *laughing settles.* **Racheal** *backs off from the table.*

Jonathan   I don't think it were painful or nothing. Didn't even notice at first. He just stopped breathing. Pulse stopped. You all right?

Racheal   Yeah.

Jonathan   You done yer homework?

Racheal   Yeah.

Jonathan   What about you, Billy?

Billy   Didn't get none.

Jonathan   Didn't yer?

Billy   No.

Jonathan   Right.

Pause.

Maybe you should go and see him. Yer can if yer want to. I think he'd have liked yer to.

Racheal   No thank you.

Silence.

Jonathan   What did Ronald say to yer?

Racheal   Nothing.

Jonathan   He's a funny cunt int 'e? Mind you. Good of him to come and that. He liked your grandad. Remember that time he brought him round?

Racheal   What?

Jonathan   Maybe you weren't there. One time. Fucking freezing cold outside. Middle of winter. Knock on the door. It were Ronald. Holding your grandad up. Under his arm and that. Grandad's got his pants round his ankles. Reckon he was having a piss. Fell over and that. In the ice. Apparently loads of people walked past him. Ronald stopped to help him back.

Racheal (*defiant*)   He never.

Jonathan (*matter-of-fact*)   He did, love. Used to do it quite a lot. Could barely fucking walk half the time. He was never that big a man. Everybody said that he was but it weren't true. You with me? He was as much of a fuck as anything else. (*Drinks.*) You been behaving yerselves?

Billy   Yeah.

Jonathan   Yer better. You done yer homework properly, Racheal? Have yer, love?

Racheal   Yes.

Jonathan   Don't want fucking aggro, do we? Got to do your homework as well as yer can. Don't want to have to go up and see no teachers. Not unless it's Miss Ayling, eh? I'd go up and see her any time. Day or night. You wiv me? (*Finishes his coffee.*) So. What are you gonna do now, Rache? Eh?

Racheal   What do you mean?

Jonathan   Got nowhere to go to now, have you, love? Monday nights and that. Tuesdays. Wednesdays. Weekends. (*Screws up his coffee cup and throws it away.*) All the time she was round there, weren't she, Bill?

Billy Yeah.

Jonathan Can't do that any more. Can yer?

Racheal It's your fault.

Jonathan You what?

Racheal This. Grandad dying. It's your fault.

Jonathan (*with a chuckle*) What yer going on about, you, eh?

Racheal Fucking bastard.

Jonathan (*shouting, suddenly*) Eh!

Racheal If you hadn't been such a fucking bastard he would have been all right.

Jonathan What you nattering on about, you, eh? What she nattering on about, Billy?

Billy Don't know.

Racheal He told us. He used to tell us. What you did. To Mum.

Jonathan Racheal. Enough. Now. Shut it.

Racheal (*starting to cry*) Told us it used to break his heart. Yer fucking bastard.

Jonathan You don't shut it now I'll fucking leather yer.

Racheal *stands, offers herself to her dad for a battering.*

Racheal (*becoming hysterical*) Yeah? Would yer? Go on then! Fucking go on! Hit us! Hit us! Go on! I'd love it. I'd love it. Yer fucking bastard!

Her hysteria collapses into sobbing for a short time and eventually calms down. **Jonathan** *watches her simply and quietly, allowing her to calm.* **Billy** *stares down at his homework.*

Jonathan (*simply, quietly*) Should go and see him.

Racheal No.

Jonathan   Should do.

Racheal   I don't want to.

Jonathan   How come not?

Racheal   Scares me.

Jonathan   What does?

Racheal   People being dead. All that.

Jonathan (*with a gentle smile*)   Don't be daft.

Racheal   I'm not being daft. I'm being serious.

Jonathan (*moving to her*)   Racheal. It's all right. You know? He won't bite yer. You should. You'd feel better for it. It'd make it a bit, y'know. Go on. I'll look after Billy. You go.

She stares at him for a short time and then leaves. He watches her go. There is a silence between **Jonathan** *and* **Billy** *for a while. The two don't look at each other.*

Billy   Dad.

Jonathan   Yeah.

Billy   Can I nick a can of Fanta Orange. Out of the fridge. They won't do out.

Jonathan (*sitting*)   Aye. All right.

He does. Comes back to the table and drinks with relish. His dad watches him for a while before speaking to him. This time, when the two address one another, they start to hold eye contact.

How are you, Bill?

Billy   Yer what?

Jonathan   Are you all right and everything? About Grandad and that?

Billy   Yeah.

Jonathan (*looking away for a bit*)   Your mum should have been here. Weren't even my dad. I held his hand. It were weird.

Billy   Dad.

Jonathan   Billy.

Billy   I don't think it were you. Who killed Grandad or nothing. I think it was all the fags he smoked. He was always smoking, him. Like a big old chimney.

Jonathan   I think so too.

Billy   Stupid. Smoking.

Jonathan   Yes it is.

Billy   Racheal smokes.

Jonathan   Does she?

Billy   All the time.

Jonathan   I see. Is she all right?

Billy   Yer what?

Jonathan   Racheal. Is she all right? Do you think?

Billy   Yeah. I think so.

Pause.

Jonathan   Billy.

Billy   Yeah.

Jonathan   I'm sorry, mate.

Billy   What about? (*Beat.*) Dad?

Jonathan   Just. Yer know.

Barely perceptibly, he starts to cry.

Look at me. Big stupid git. Crying and that.

Long silence. The two look away from each other. **Jonathan** *still only just crying.*

Racheal *comes back before* **Jonathan** *notices. Stands by the table. She catches him crying. He realises she has caught him. A vulnerable moment and then he inhales a big lungful of air.*

Racheal   You all right? Dad?

Jonathan   I'm fine love, yeah. You OK?

Racheal   Yeah.

Jonathan (*smiling at her*)   Good girl. It weren't too bad. Was it?

Racheal   No. It was all right.

Jonathan (*standing*)   He was a funny fucker. Said to us. This morning. Tell Racheal and Billy that when I get better, we'll go out. Go to KFC. Go cinema.

Racheal   His skin was very loose.

Jonathan   Yer what?

Racheal   On his bones. It was warm. Yer press the skin down though and the muscles and the bone are all cold. It was weird.

Jonathan   Yeah.

He picks up **Billy**'s *coat. Neatens the collar. Passes it to him.*

You wanna go home, you two?

Racheal   Yeah.

Jonathan   See y'up at car.

Jonathan *exits.* **Billy** *follows.*

Billy (*leaving*)   Starving.

Racheal *goes to leave. Stops herself. Looks back.*

Lights dim.

Racheal *pushes down her school socks. Removes her tie and reties it in a fat knot. Pulls her skirt up, tightens it slightly. Applies some make-up. Ties her jumper round her waist.*

Scene Three

1992. The L section of the bus station in Stockport town centre. It is approaching night-time and darkening. The station is deserted except for the children. It feels huge, almost completely hollow. The children's movement is freed by the absence of others.

An aluminium queue divider centres the stage.

Racheal Keats, *fifteen years old, leans against the divider's pole. Breathless. Waiting.*

Chris Bennett, *also fifteen years old, follows her. Not breathless. In a tracksuit. Cocky, confident, very handsome and knows it. He joins her, leaning against the pole. Looks at her for some time without speaking. She grows increasingly self-conscious of this.*

They are waiting for their friends. He watches her while she talks. She can't look back.

Racheal   Gonna rain. Bet ya.

Chris   –

Racheal   Gonna slash it down.

Chris   –

Racheal *moves away from the pole – looks outwards and all around her.*

Racheal   Always rainin' here. Always fuckin' leatherin' it.

Chris   –

Racheal   Fuckin' hate it.

Chris (*laughs briefly*)   –

Racheal   Don't you, Chris?

Chris (*smiles*)   What?

Racheal   Don't you hate it here?

Chris (*thinks, sniffs*)   S'arright.

Racheal   S'fuckin' never. S'fucking cheap. Grotty. Shit buildings. Stinks. (*She belches hugely and then giggles.*)

Chris (*with a grin*)   Yer got a tab?

Racheal   No.

Chris   Liar.

Racheal   Am not.

Chris   Y'are. Fuckin' seen ya. Juss now.

Racheal   Finished 'em.

Chris   Yer didn't. Yer still got some.

Racheal   I ain't.

He reaches for her shirt pocket. Slight scuffle. Giggle.

Chris   Here.

Racheal   Get off.

Chris   In yer pocket.

Racheal   Get off us.

He pulls out a packet of cigarettes.

Chris   Told ya.

Racheal   'S me last one.

Chris   Yer cheeky little monkey. Knew y'ad one.

He puts it in his mouth. Goes to light it. She grabs for it. Misses.

Racheal   Don't.

He backs away from her, always watching her, grinning.

Chris   Stop me.

Racheal   Chris.

Chris   Come on.

Racheal   What are yer like?

Chris   If yer don't want me to smoke it come and gerrit off me.

Racheal   Yer mental.

Chris   Am not.

Racheal   Yer crackers.

Chris   Am not. Am well sane.

He lights the cigarette.

Racheal   Loony.

Chris   Look at yer. Yer all red. Yer look dead cute when yer all red.

Racheal (*affectionately*)   Cracked you.

Chris *takes a long draw on the cigarette. They stare at each other for a time.*

Racheal (*turning from him, out into space*)   Only good things around here are Man U. And Mr Everson.

Chris   Mr Everson?

Racheal   Yeah.

Chris   He's a fat fucking thick twat.

Racheal   He's not. He's fucking great.

Chris   Yer fancy him, don't yer? Fucking hell.

Racheal   No. I just think he's good.

Chris   You fucking fancy him and all.

Racheal   Teaches us new words.

Chris   New words?

Racheal   Catatonic. A state of schizophrenic unconsciousness.

Chris   New words? Are you eight?

Racheal   Philanthropy. Love of mankind. (*Suddenly turns to him.*) Yer know what else I love?

Chris   What?

Racheal   All mountains.

Chris   Yer what?

Racheal   Our mum went on about them all the time and all. Yer should've seen 'em this morning. Such a clear day. Yer could see 'em all really detailed. We should go. Shouldn't we? Me and you. Tek Luce and Danny.

Chris   Tek your kid.

Racheal   Fuck off.

Chris   I like him.

Racheal   Yer can have him.

Chris   He's a nutter. Nicks out, don't he?

Racheal   What?

Chris   Billy. Nicks out. 'S funny. Like 'avin' a lickle dog.

Silence.

'S not mountains. 'S fuckin' hills. 'S fuckin' Pennine Way that. 'S never fuckin' mountains.

Racheal   Yer ever noticed how many transport routes cut through this place?

Chris   Yer what?

Racheal   All the transport routes come through here. Every single fuckin' type.

Chris   What yer crackin' on about now, you?

She begins to circle away from him.

Racheal   Yer got yer A6 for yer cars. Yer got yer viaduct for yer trains. M62. River fuckin' Mersey. Flight paths down Ringway. 'S mental. Planes have still got the wheels down when they come over here. Every cunt's trying to get out.

Chris   Am not.

Racheal   Int yer?

Chris   Nah.

Racheal (*to him*)   Int yer, Chris? Really?

Chris   No.

Racheal (*turning away, staring out again*)   Fuckin' should.

Chris   I like it.

Racheal   Why?

Chris   'S a laugh, innit? Yer can bunk off school. Go home. Watch telly. Brother's all right. Mum and Dad and that. Phone yer mates. Come down here. Ride buses. Go down Manchester. Go cinema. Gerr up to all sorts.

Racheal (*turning to him, seriously*)   I hate my family.

Chris   No yer don't.

Racheal   The only person in my family who's any cop was my grandad and he's been dead two year. Most significant person in my life and he's fucking snuffed it.

Chris   Yer brother's all right.

Pause. **Racheal** *stares out.*

Racheal   I hate death. Scares the shit out of us.

Pause.

Remember Paul Castle?

Chris   Yeah.

Racheal   Remember his brother?

Chris   His brother?

Racheal   In third year. When we was in first year. Threw himself off bridge over M62. Remember that?

Chris   Oh yeah.

Racheal   I remember thinkin' it were funny. And that he were stupid. That he were a thick cunt. I mean, as if yer do that. We're older than he was now. Paul Castle's older than his older brother. Nuts that, int it?

Chris (*disinterested*)   Yeah.

Racheal   It is though, Chris, int it?

Chris   I used to like Paul Castle. He were all right. How come he never comes to school any more?

She looks at him for three seconds. Looks away.

Racheal   I don't know.

Pause. She looks back to him. He begins to lift his own weight up off the bar. And then stops.

Chris   Yer know one thing I like about you?

Racheal   What?

Chris   You've got really great tits.

Racheal   Yer what?

Chris   Y'ave. They look great.

Racheal   Do they?

Chris   Yeah.

Racheal   Right.

Chris   Don't panic. It's a good thing.

Racheal   Thanks.

Chris   'S all right.

He turns away again, grinning.

Racheal   Where are they?

Chris   Don't know.

Pause.

Racheal   Chris.

Chris   Yeah.

Racheal   What are you scared of?

Chris   How do yer mean?

Racheal   Like I'm scared of death. And when I were a
nipper I were scared of me mum when she used to thump us
with her hairbrush and me dad because he was fucking
weird. What are you scared of?

Chris   Nothing.

Racheal   Nothing?

Chris   No.

She touches his face with her finger. Pulls it away.

Racheal (*seriously*)   Liar.

Chris   Am not.

Racheal   Yer are.

Long pause. Neither shakes eye contact.

Racheal   Y'ever get like yer just want to go fucking ape?

Chris   Yer what?

Racheal   Don't matter.

She turns away from him. The two stare out. **Billy** *runs on. He is ten
years old.*

Billy   That was fuckin' magic!

Racheal   Billy.

Billy   That was fuckin' brilliant!

Racheal   What?

Billy   That!

Racheal   What?

Billy   We just went down Merseyway. Fuckin' robbin' and everything! It were top!

Racheal   Yer what?

Billy   Just down Boots and that.

Racheal   Boots's closed.

Billy   Smashed the window.

Chris *bursts out laughing.* **Racheal** *is appalled.*

Racheal   You what?!?

Billy   Me and Luce and Danny.

Racheal   Billy.

Billy   Threw a big fuckin' brick through the window. Grabbed a load of films for cameras. And skin cream. And pegged it. Alarms going. (*Imitating the sound of the alarm.*) BLAH BLAH BLAH BLAH!!

As **Billy** *talks he moves like a monkey. Swinging on the queue divider. Circling the stage. He hardly stops moving at all.*

Racheal   Billy, I am going to fucking kill you.

Billy   It were magic. It were mighty!

Chris   Where's Luce now, Billy? And Danny?

Billy   They're coming. Slow fuckers. Am a dead fast runner, me. Fuckin' slaughtered 'em.

Racheal   What the fuck did you do that for, Billy? Christ!

Billy   For a laugh.

Racheal   Yer don't need skin cream!

Billy   I nicked it for you. Lucy's got some and all.

He gives her six bottles of skin cream that he pulls out of his pockets.

Racheal   I don't want this!

Billy   Why not?

Racheal   Fuckin' handling stolen, int it?

She refuses to take them.

Billy   But I nicked it for you. And look at these. Fuckin top these are. Fuckin' quality.

He pulls out a handful of boxes of film.

Racheal   Billy. You haven't even got a camera. What do yer want film for, yer mong head?

Billy   Fuck off.

Racheal   No, Billy –

Billy   Am not a mong head.

Racheal   It's not on.

Billy   Don't call me a mong head, Rache, because I'm fucking not one, arright?

Racheal   Billy.

Billy   What?

Racheal   Dad'll kill you.

Billy   He won't.

Racheal   He fucking will.

Billy   Don't need to tell him.

Racheal   I *know*.

Billy   Don't need to tell him nothing. Gissa fag.

Racheal   Fuck off.

Billy   Go on. Am gasping.

Racheal   Billy. You do my head in.

Billy   Anyways. What's all this?

Racheal   All what?

Billy   All you two. What's all this about?

Racheal   Shut it.

Billy   Give im one, did ya?

Racheal   Billy.

Billy   Honestly, Chris. You should hear her going on about you. She really fancies yer. She'd definitely give yer one. If yer wanted. Just ask her.

Racheal   Right, Billy.

Billy   She's always going with lads and all. She's a right slapper.

Racheal *gives* **Billy** *a Chinese burn. He buckles in pain.*

Racheal   Take that back.

Billy   I was joking.

Racheal   I don't care. Take it back.

Billy   It was a joke, Rache.

Racheal   It wasn't a fucking funny one. Take it fucking back.

Billy   I'm sorry.

Racheal   Take it back.

Chris (*amused*)   You should take it back, Billy.

Racheal   Keep out of this, you!

Billy   Arright. I take it back. I'm sorry. I take it back.

Racheal (*letting* **Billy** *go*)   Nothing to do with you. To do with me and him.

Chris (*slight laugh*)   Sorry. I was just trying to help.

Racheal   Yeah. Well, just don't.

Lucy *and* **Danny** *enter running.* **Lucy** *is fifteen. School uniform worn like* **Racheal***'s. Pretty. Slightly softer than* **Racheal***.* **Danny** *is in messy school uniform too.* **Lucy** *is laughing.* **Danny** *fretting slightly.*

Lucy   Oh my fucking lord!

Danny   I can't breathe.

Lucy   Racheal. Your brother is a fucking lunatic.

Danny   I've never known anything like it.

Racheal   What did he do?

Lucy   He is off his head. I swear.

Racheal   What did he do, Lucy?

Lucy   He wants to go up Dollis Hill. He wants to go in' fuckin loony bin.

Racheal   Lucy, what did he fucking do?

Lucy   Only threw a brick in window of fucking Boots is all. Only did that, didn't he?

Danny   Racheal. He's cracked. Am telling yer.

As **Lucy** *talks,* **Billy***'s movements calm. He is very proud of himself.* **Lucy** *cracks into laughter as she speaks.*

Lucy   Juss walking down Merseyway. Went into McDonald's and going down Merseyway. Just having us chips. And he just turns round with this fucking great brick and he just lobs it into window of fucking Boots. Grabs all these, all these, all these fucking films and skin cream and that and just fucking pegs it. He's off his fucking head. He wants to go to fucking hospital. What does he want fucking skin cream for? I swear. It were brilliant.

Billy   I gave you some.

Racheal   Lucy.

Lucy   Yeah. You did, love. It were very sweet of you. I nearly pissed myself.

Danny   Alarms going and everything.

Billy (*going to* **Lucy**)   It were good though, weren't it?

Danny   Cops coming now, I reckon, probly.

Billy   Lucy, weren't it good though?

Lucy   Eh?

Billy   Doing that. It were good, weren't it?

Lucy (*strokes his face, he beams*)   Yeah. Yes, love. It were fucking cracking.

Racheal   You mean it wasn't your idea?

Lucy   Yer what?

Billy   Am gonna do it again.

Racheal   Robbing shop. Robbing Boots. It wasn't your idea to do that?

Lucy   No. First I heard about it he's got the brick in his hands and he's going, 'Watch this!'

Billy   What you reckon, Danny, should we do it again?

Danny   What?

Billy   Go and do JD Sports. Get some trainers.

Racheal   Billy, I need a word with you.

Billy   Get us a football.

Danny   Are you mental?

Racheal   Billy. Now.

Billy   Fuck off.

Danny   Cops'll be fucking crawling all over this place. They'll be after yer. Get yer on camera and that.

Billy   Will they fuck!

Danny   They will, Billy.

Billy   Be the last thing they expect then, eh? Go back and nick stuff from right in front of 'em. Fucking thick coppers.

Lucy   He's a lunatic.

Chris (*grinning, watchful*)   I'll go.

Billy   Excellent!

Racheal (*staring at* **Chris**)   I don't believe this.

Chris   You coming, Danny?

Danny   What?

Chris   You coming with us or what?

Danny   No chance.

Racheal   Chris, don't.

Chris (*big grin, loving it*)   Chicken.

Danny   Fuck off.

Chris   Fucking ten-year-old got more balls than you do.

Danny   I was fucking there just then, weren't I? Don't know where you were.

Chris   Fucking coward. Int he, Rache? He's a fucking coward.

Danny   I just done fucking Boots me, mate.

Chris   Yer never. Billy did fucking Boots. You just stood there. That's not doing it. That's just fucking coincidence is what that is. Yer a fucking pussy.

Danny   Fuck off.

Chris   Fucking pussy. You coming, Lucy?

Lucy   Me?

Chris   Aye.

Pause.

Lucy   Just let us get me breath back.

Chris   Good girl.

Billy   You coming Rache?

Racheal (*she looks at* **Chris**, *appalled, and then addresses* **Billy**) You're not going anywhere.

Billy   Yeah I am. Me and Chris and Lucy are going robbing JD Sports. We're going getting trainers. You coming too, Danny?

Danny   I don't know, mate.

Chris   He's fucking chicken. 'S what he is.

Danny   'S not chicken. 'S never chicken, arright? 'S fucking mental is what it is!

Racheal   Chris, please.

Chris   What? Rache? Yer never going mard-arsed on us and all, are yer?

Lucy   She fucking is, int she? What's she fucking like?

Billy *goes to leave.*

Racheal   Billy. Wait here.

Billy   No. Am going. You coming or what?

Racheal   This is doing my nut in.

Billy   Rache?

Racheal   You can't take him, Chris. He's my brother. He's only ten.

Billy   So?!

Chris (*with real relish*)   Mard arse.

Lucy *laughs at* **Racheal**.

Billy   God, Racheal.

Danny   Yer shouldn't, Chris.

Chris   Shut it, chicken shit.

The two face off. Brief time. **Danny** *looks away.*

Billy *drops the face cream on the floor as he starts to go.*

Racheal   This int right.

Billy (*turning to her as he goes*)   Am not a fucking kid any more.

Racheal   Yes you are.

Billy (*stops, stares at her briefly, sniffs once*)   Am going.

He turns and leaves.

Chris   Me too. (*Goes to leave.*) Coming Danny?

Danny (*after a brief beat, and with great reluctance*)   Aye. Yeah. Am coming. Fuck.

Chris   You wanna sort your head, Rache. Yer wiv me? It's turning fucking yellow, mate.

Leaves. **Danny** *follows* **Billy** *and* **Chris** *off.* **Racheal** *watches them go. Turns away. Looks out. Wraps her arms around herself. Brief time.* **Lucy** *goes right up to her.*

Lucy   So?

Racheal   What?

Lucy   Did you?

Racheal   What?

Lucy   You and Chris? Did yer do it with him?

Racheal *simply stares at her for a few seconds.*

Lucy   Yer did, didn't yer? I knew it!

Pause. She stares at **Racheal** *with a wonder that edges on to disgust.* **Racheal** *turns away from her.*

You coming?

Racheal   I don't believe this.

Lucy   You coming or what?

Racheal   I hate this.

Lucy   Racheal, are you coming with us or fucking what?

No response.

Used to be arright you and all, I thought.

Lucy *leaves.* **Racheal** *watches her go and then stands.*

Lights dim.

Racheal *takes off her tie. Tucks in her shirt. Takes off her shoes and socks. Puts on a light, summer cardigan, maybe some sunglasses.*

Scene Four

1994. The garden of a nursing home in Offerton, Stockport.
    A wrought-iron bench. Some flowerpots. It is a beautiful day. There is golden sunshine. A bright, warm, open light.
    Racheal Keats, *seventeen, tends the plants in the pots. Afterwards she walks, relaxed, around the bench. Her nana,* **Anne Dickinson**, *sits still on the bench.*
    Anne *is seventy-four years old. She is blind. She wears a powder-blue cardigan over a white dress. Her ankles are thick and rolled in brown tights and bandages.* **Anne** *is recovering from a stroke. Her temperament is resolutely cheery. Sometimes the tone of her voice is inappropriately, confusingly cheery.*
    They are drinking tea from china cups and eating a huge block of Dairy Milk chocolate.
    We can hear birdsong. Perhaps cars. And offstage we can hear the sound of an old **Man** *howling from an open window.*

Man What am I doing here? What am I here for? I've never done nothing. I've not done out. Please. Please. Please. Please. Please. Please. Please. Please. Please. Please don't. Please don't do that. Please stop doing that. Please stop.

They stop to listen for a while. After a short while the window is slammed closed. They both stare out.

Racheal Nana? Who was that?

Anne Who?

Racheal That man. Him shouting.

Anne What man?

Racheal Did you not hear him. That fellah. Shouting on he was. Going crackers and everything?

Anne No.

Racheal He was shouting like mad.

Anne Oh. I don't know.

Pause. They look out. **Racheal** *checks her watch.*

Racheal It's a beautiful day, Nana.

Anne Yes. It feels it.

Racheal (*looking at the sky*) The sky's very blue.

Anne Is it?

Racheal It looks amazing.

Anne Does it?

Racheal Sun's out. Couple of clouds and that. All white. Very little.

Anne I love it when there's a little breeze.

Racheal Yeah. Me too.

Anne It smells like artichokes.

Racheal   Artichokes?

Anne   And tea. The air. From when I was a little girl and everything.

Pause.

Racheal   Do yer want some more chocolate?

Anne   Yes. I do please.

She cracks off a large chunk and passes it to her. Her nana starts biting on the large chunk.

Racheal   Nana, there was something I wanted to ask you.

Anne   Does it no good.

Racheal   What?

Anne   My teeth.

Racheal   No. (*Beat.*) Nana.

Anne   How are you, love?

Racheal   You what?

Anne   How are you? Are you all right? Is everything all right? With you?

Racheal   Yes. It's fine. I'm good. I'm all right. It's all right.

Anne   How's your brother?

Racheal   Billy?

Anne   Yes. Billy. How is he?

Racheal   He's not bad. Have you been to see him?

Anne   Have I what?

Racheal   Have you been to see him? Billy?

Anne   No. No I've not.

Racheal   You should go.

Anne   I've not.

Beat. **Racheal** *turns to her.*

Racheal   Have yer seen Mum, Nana?

Anne   Have I what?

Racheal   Mum. Have you seen her?

Anne   No. I haven't.

Racheal   Do you know where she's gone?

Anne   No, I don't. Do you?

Racheal   No. I've no idea.

Anne   Yer what?

Racheal   I said I've no idea.

Anne   No.

Racheal (*moves to sit on the arm of the bench*)   Can I ask you something, Nana?

Anne   What love?

Racheal   Don't you miss her?

Anne   Who?

Racheal   Mum.

Anne (*smiling*)   Yes. I do.

Racheal   Doesn't it make you sad? That she's gone away and she never even said goodbye or nothing. She just left.

Anne (*smiling*)   Yes it does.

Racheal   I always wondered. It's been ages now. I always wondered if she wrote to you. Or spoke to you on the telephone. Or come to see you.

Anne (*smiling*)   No she didn't.

Pause. **Racheal** *stares at her.*

Racheal   Do you miss Grandad ever?

Anne   What did you say, love?

Racheal   I asked you if you ever missed Grandad?

Anne   No. No I don't. No.

Racheal   I miss him all the time.

Pause. **Racheal** *stands, moves away.*

Anne   Have you got a boyfriend yet?

Racheal   No. Nana. I haven't.

Long pause. She tends the plants again. Then stops. Stares at her nana.

Racheal   Nana. I'm going to get a flat.

Anne   Are you, love?

Racheal   Up Edgely.

Anne   That's nice.

Racheal   I'm dead excited.

Anne   Are you?

Racheal   I am. It's really smart. It's got a bathroom. Kitchen. Got a shower.

Anne   Has it?

Racheal   It's cracking. Rent's thirty quid a week. I can afford that. It's all right.

Anne   Good girl.

Racheal   Nana. I need some money. For the deposit. I need two hundred and forty pound. For the deposit, which is a month's rent, and for a month's rent in advance. Nana, I've not got it. I can't afford the deposit. I was going to ask you. If you had it. If I could borrow it from you. If you could lend it to us.

Anne   Were you?

Racheal   Yeah.

Pause.

Can you, Nana?

Anne   Can I what?

Racheal   Can you lend us the deposit? The two hundred and forty pound?

Anne (*smiling*)   No, love, I don't think so.

Racheal   Yer what?

Anne   I don't think I can love, no.

Racheal   Nana? Did you hear what I said? I've not got it. If I don't get the deposit and the rent then I'll lose the flat. I'll pay you back. I will, Nana, I swear. On my life. I'll pay you back. Every month. I could pay you like twenty quid a month or summit. I could do that. I could afford that. Nana. On my life.

Anne (*smiling*)   I don't think so, love. No.

Racheal   What do you mean you don't think so?

Anne   I don't think I could lend you the money, love, not really.

Racheal   Why not?

Anne   I haven't really got enough, love.

Racheal   Yer what?

Anne   I haven't. I can't really afford to do that.

Silence. **Racheal** *stares at her nana, disbelieving. She eats some more chocolate.*

I've not got the money.

Racheal   I thought, Mum always said you were . . . didn't Grandad leave you any?

Anne   I'm sorry, love?

Racheal   Didn't Grandad, I thought – Grandad always said there was some money . . .

Anne   No, love.

Racheal   He always said, he told me, Grandad told me that there was some money and if that, if I ever needed some money badly that he would find it for me and he would lend it to me. He told me. He promised. (*Beat.*) Yer must have it.

Anne   Love, I don't.

Racheal   How do you, how do you, how do yer afford to pay for this place if you've not got any money, Nana?

Anne   Yer what?

Racheal   How can you afford to pay for this place if you've not got any money to lend us?

Anne   It's not easy, love.

Racheal   Not easy?

Anne   No, love.

Racheal   Grandad promised me.

Anne   It's not, love.

Racheal   I need that flat, Nana. I need it. Dad's, Dad's, Dad's, Dad's . . . I'll crack up. If I don't get that flat, Nana, I will go mental. I swear.

Anne   You won't.

Racheal   I will, Nana. I really will.

Anne   Is there any more chocolate, love?

Racheal   Grandad said.

Anne   Is there? Could you pass me some?

Racheal   I could pay you back thirty a month. If that's what's bothering you. Nana, please. I need this so much.

Anne   You wouldn't.

Racheal   What?

Anne   You wouldn't, love. Would you? Not really. You never would.

Racheal   You what?

Anne   Would you?

Racheal   I don't believe this.

Anne   Would you though, love? You wouldn't. Would you?

Racheal   I don't believe this one bit. I swear.

Anne   Racheal, sweetheart, is there any more chocolate?

Racheal   Don't call me sweetheart. You're not. I'm not your sweetheart.

Anne   Is there, love?

Racheal   You have no idea. Do you?

Anne   Yer what, love?

Racheal   Yer lying.

Anne   Yer what, love?

Racheal   You heard me. You can hear me perfectly well. Yer lying. Yer lying about yer ears and yer lying about yer money. Yer a lickle liar.

Anne   Racheal, love. I'm not, I swear.

Racheal   I'll give yer some more chocolate. Here y'are.

Passes her a chunk of chocolate that she puts in her mouth.

Here, Nana, have some more.

Gives her some more chocolate, which she holds in her hand.

Have some more.

Anne   I can't hold any more, love. I can't fit it in my mouth.

Racheal   Have some more chocolate, you skinny fucking tramp.

Anne   Racheal, please.

Racheal   Have it. Have it. Have it. Have it. Have it. I'll kick your teeth in.

Anne *takes some more. Puts some more in her mouth. Her mouth is full. Dribbles of chocolate on her chin.*

Racheal   Have some more.

The same. **Anne** *can't talk. She's crying.*

Is it good being you, Nana? Is it good being a cripple? What about pissing all the time, is that good? Does it hurt? Do your legs hurt when you piss on them? Do they? Do you think –

Anne   Christine?

Racheal   Do you think, Nana – I'm not Christine, you blind – Nana, do you think you're going to die soon? Do you, Nana? Do you think you are?

Anne   Where's Christine gone? Where is she?

Racheal   She's not here. She's gone. She left you. She left you because she couldn't stand you.

Anne   Christine?

Racheal   Her and Grandad. Both of them. Yer blind fuck.

Racheal *picks up her nana's handbag. Pulls things out from it. Tissues. Sweets. Pills. A make-up compact. Her purse. She opens the purse and pulls out two or three ten-pound notes and a handful of change and holds them in her hand.*

Anne   Christine? What are you doing, love?

Racheal *stares at her nana for some time. Appalled by the chocolate, the spittle, the tears, the money. Appalled by what she has done perhaps.*

Racheal (*gulping her breath*)   Nana. What's the saddest thing that ever happened to you? What is it? Do you think?

Anne   My daughter's gone. She went. She's gone.

Racheal   Can yer blame her though, really, can yer?

Anne   I feel sick.

Racheal   Stick yer fingers down yer throat. Make yer feel better.

Anne   I don't know who you are.

Racheal   Yer what?

Anne   I don't know who you are.

Racheal *drops the handbag on the floor. Stares at the money and at her nana for three seconds.*

Lights dim.

Racheal *takes off her sunglasses. Watches her nana leave. Waits.*

Scene Five

1996. The staffroom of the Somerfield's supermarket, Heaton Moor Road, Heaton Moor, Stockport.
   Early evening autumn light coming in from a small window.
   There are two sets of lockers at opposite sides of the stage. Each have a clipboard hanging from them with timesheets and a pen attached.
   In the centre of the stage there is a double-sided bench divided by a row of hooks. Normally the coats on these hooks would divide the staffroom more obviously into a girls' changing area and a boys' changing area but now there are no coats. The demeanour of the characters should still, however, delineate the gender of the areas.
   *Before the lights rise, **Racheal** puts her cardigan in her locker and puts on a green Somerfield's uniform. She is getting changed*

out of her uniform. She will take trainers and socks from out of the locker.

Lights rise. **Danny Miller**, *aged nineteen, stands perfectly still, quite rigid, in the boys' half. He has just been punched by a shoplifter. His eye is bruised. His contact lens has become dislodged.* **Racheal Keats**, *also nineteen, holds his eye open and is trying to prise the lens from underneath his eyelid.*

Danny *has nurtured and developed the combination of boyish charm and guarded caution that we saw in Scene Three. He is a handsome boy now. He too is wearing a Gateway's uniform.*

Danny   Careful.

Racheal   I'm being careful.

Danny   It kills that.

Racheal   Shut up. Keep still.

Danny   I'm keeping still, aren't I?

Racheal   Danny.

Danny   How fucking still do you want me to be?

Racheal   You keep blinking. Don't swear.

Danny   You're sticking your fingers in my eye. Of course I keep blinking. Fuck's sake.

Racheal   Danny!

She spots the lens and starts to move it out of the eyelid.

Hold on. I see it. Steady. Steady. Steady.

Danny   Rache.

Racheal (*succeeding*)   Got it.

Danny (*folding back*)   Arrrgghh.

Racheal *hands him the lens, which he takes.*

Racheal   Say thank you, Racheal.

Danny   Jesus. That was sore.

Racheal   Danny.

Danny   Thank you, Racheal.

Racheal   Wash that. Before you put it back in.

Danny *looks around. Finds nothing to wash it with.* **Racheal**
returns to the girls' side. **Danny** *spits on the contact lens. Puts the
lens back in his eye.* **Racheal** *takes off her overall and puts it in the
locker, folding it while she talks. Takes out socks and trainers, which
she puts on, and a coat. Checks her hair in a mirror in her locker door.
Maybe brushes it. Maybe applies some deodorant. All while she talks
to* **Danny**.

Racheal   That was weird. Touching your eyeball. It felt
much harder than you'd have thought.

Danny   Thank you for getting it out.

Racheal   That's all right. Did he hurt you?

Danny   No. Just caught us. Right on the lens and that.
Couldn't get to it. It does your head in a bit.

Racheal   He was a poor bastard, wa'n't he?

Danny   Police come yet?

Racheal   Just now. He were crying. Did you see?

Danny   Serves him right.

Racheal   Reckoned they'd send him down. Done it
before, he said.

Danny   Fucking tuna fish. Brainy fella, eh?

Racheal (*grinning*)   You looked very funny running after
him.

Danny (*grinning back*)   Fuck off.

Racheal   Your legs were all mad. Flapping out behind
you.

Danny   Fuck off.

Racheal   Run like a girl.

Danny   Rache.

Racheal   What?

Danny   Shut it.

Racheal (*with a giggle, interrupting her changing, going to peer round into his side*)   Or what?

Danny   Or . . . just . . .

They hold each other's eyes for a long moment. Smiling. Both of them on the point of saying something. Neither speaking. Eventually:

You look beautiful. Even in uniform and that. You do.

Racheal   Thank you.

Danny   Uniform's hanging. Makes most people look like spastics. But it don't bother me on you.

Racheal   That's good. You look like a knob in yours.

Danny *takes his shoes off and wipes dirt from them. Breathes on them. Polishes them. While he talks to* **Racheal** *he hardly looks at her. Concentrating deeply on the cleaning of the shoes. She goes back to her side, continues to change. He starts to talk quite quietly. As though he is afraid somebody might overhear him. Nobody would.*

Danny   Last night. (*Beat.*) It was good, wasn't it? It was all right. I liked it.

Racheal   Me too.

Danny   I was worried when I got up this morning. Just looking at you and that. I was worried that you might have thought that you'd made a big mistake or summit. Y'know what I mean?

Racheal   I didn't.

Danny   I was trying to figure out if you were really asleep or if you were just pretending to be asleep so that I'd leave.

Racheal   I wasn't.

Danny   No. I know. You started snoring.

Racheal   I never.

Danny   Yer did. Like a little baby pig.

Racheal *sticks her tongue out at him.*

Danny   I like your flat.

Racheal   Thanks.

Danny   It's smart. Yer lucky.

Racheal   I know.

Danny   Good area Edgely. I reckon.

Racheal   It's all right.

Danny   How much you paying?

Racheal   Thirty quid a week.

Danny   'S all right that, int it?

Racheal   Working here. It's easy.

Danny   How d'yer get the deposit?

Racheal   Saved up.

Danny   Do you like it? Living on your own?

Racheal   I love it.

Danny   Don't you miss your Billy? Or your dad or nothing.

Racheal   No. I see Billy most days. I never saw much of Dad anyway.

Beat. Looks at **Danny** *before she speaks.*

You know when you think of somebody?

Danny   Yer what?

Racheal   Like if you had a mental picture of somebody. When you close your eyes and you think of them just off the top of yer head.

Danny   Yeah?

Racheal   When I do that with my dad I can only ever see him down the pub. I can't imagine him in our flat. At all. I can't get it in my head. In the pub. Or in hospital.

Danny   In hospital?

Racheal   In the café there. Don't matter. It got to the point when I couldn't actually stand the way they smelled. The way the flat smelled. The way our dad ate apples. Did my head in.

Danny   How's your Billy doing?

Racheal   He's all right. Glad to be home. Reckons he's going to keep himself out of bother and that now. We'll see eh?

Danny   You reckon he'd remember us?

Racheal   Course. He used to like you.

Danny   Say hello to him for us, eh?

Racheal   I will do, yeah.

She comes round to the boys' side and sits on the bench and looks at him.

Can I ask you a question?

Danny   Go on.

Racheal   Does it bother you that we didn't have sex last night?

Danny   No.

Racheal   Are you sure?

Danny   Course I am.

Racheal   Yer not lying?

Danny   Rache, I had, it was, I thought, it was one of the best nights I'd ever had. In my life, Rache. In my whole life, mate. Honestly.

Racheal (*with a huge smile*)   Right. Good. I just wanted to check.

She smiles at him for a few seconds. Stands up and, as she speaks, moves around exploring the boys' changing room. Trying to open **Danny**'s *and even other men's lockers. Pacing the size of the side.*

What star sign are you?

Danny   Yer what?

Racheal   What's your star sign?

Danny   Gemini, why?

Racheal   I'm trying to think of things I don't know about you.

Danny   Why?

Racheal   I just think it would be good. To know them. I'm Aquarius. That's good. Gemini and Aquarius.

Danny   Do you believe all that?

Racheal   No. Not really. Sometimes. What's your favourite colour?

Danny   (You're) Mental.

Racheal   Go on, Danny, tell us.

Danny   Why?

Racheal   Because I want to know. What is it?

Danny   Blue. What's yours?

Racheal   Indigo.

Danny   Indigo?

Racheal   What's your favourite taste?

Danny   Steak.

Racheal   Steak?

Danny   Yeah. A really nice steak. Juicy. All the blood. I love that.

Racheal   You ever had ice cream and lemonade?

Danny   Course.

Racheal   That's better. Than steak.

Danny   No it isn't

Racheal   Fucking is.

Danny (*mocking, with a gentle snort*)   Girl.

Racheal   What about clothes? What are your favourite clothes? This is good this.

She stands on the bench and walks up and down it. Kicking him out of the way when she arrives at him.

Danny   I've got a Pringle jumper that my brother got me. 'S top.

Racheal   I like shoes better than almost anything in the world.

Danny   Even better than ice cream and lemonade?

Racheal   Miles. What's your favourite smell?

Danny   Oil paint.

Racheal   You what?

Danny   Oil paint.

Racheal   You some kind of glue sniffer are you?

Danny   No. Always reminds me of primary school. Used to love it there.

Racheal   I love the way swimming pools smell. All the chlorine. And the fans on the walls outside. The way they're really warm.

Danny (*simply*)   I love the way your hair smells.

Racheal   Thank you.

Danny   That's all right.

Racheal (*watches him, jumps down, and then, after a beat*)   I really want to kiss you.

Danny   Do you?

Racheal   Like mental. Like nothing you'd ever believe.

The shop manager, **Jake Moran** *walks in. He is a short, bespectacled man. Forty-eight years old. He has short wispy hair and wears a suit. He is agitated. He distracts himself from the frankness of his apology by constantly rifling through the timesheets, attached to a clipboard which he takes down from their place hanging on the lockers, and neatening his tie as he talks. He is surprised to find* **Racheal** *in the boys' side of the changing rooms.*

Moran   Beirut. That's what it's getting like in here. It's like a war zone. It's like Beirut. All these little monkeys coming in here. Do you know, Racheal? Do you know how many, how many, how many incidents of shoplifting we've reported in the last month?

Racheal   I'm not really sure, Mr Moran, no.

Moran   Have a guess. Go on. I bet you never get it.

Racheal   Twelve.

Moran   Twenty-three. Twenty-three thieving fucking shoplifters in one fucking month. And they're just the ones we see. And report. It's not, what it's not, is, it's not reasonable. These aren't reasonable conditions under which my staff should be expected to work. Are you all right, Danny?

Danny   I'm fine, Mr Moran, honestly. I'm all right, yeah.

Moran (*concentrating on the timesheets*)   I tell Mr Ridgely. I tell him. I tell him. He makes sympathetic, well, noises. Sympathetic little noises is what he makes. But I don't think that's enough. I really, I, I really, actually, I really don't. I don't. Any more. I just don't. (*Looking straight at* **Danny**.) He could have hurt you. Couldn't he?

Danny   He wouldn't have done.

Moran   But he might have done. People get, these people, they, well, they get desperate is what they get. I'm really very sorry that this had to happen to you, Danny. I'm very grateful to you for what you did. If you want to take the rest of the afternoon off then you can do and I'll fill out your hours as normal. I'll do that. Because you shouldn't expect to deal with what you had to deal with just now. It's not . . . (*large inhalation of breath as he finds the right word*) . . . reasonable.

Danny   No. Honestly. I'll be fine.

Moran (*polishes his glasses on his shirt*)   When the police came to get him. He started whimpering. Stamped his feet. Before they got here he begged me to actually, what he did, is he begged me to let him go. Actually. Had a, a, a, a tantrum. He must have been thirty. Thirty-two. If you need anything, Danny, I'll be in my office. It leaves you breathless. Doesn't it? Sometimes?

Danny   It does, yes.

Moran   Just. Breathless. Danny. Racheal. I'll be in my office.

He leaves. They laugh affectionately. Smile at each other. Vaguely bewildered.

Racheal   Are you all right? Really?

Danny   I'm fine. Honestly.

Racheal   I wasn't worried or nothing. Watching you. My heart didn't beat any faster. It was just like watching TV. Is that bad do you think?

Danny No. Course not. (*Having tied his laces he stands.*) I should get back.

Racheal Do you have to?

Danny Got to finish stuff. Before the shift finishes. You done now?

Racheal Yeah. What time do you finish?

Danny Six.

Racheal Should I wait for you?

Danny Four hours. Don't be soft.

Racheal You could take the afternoon off. He said. Tell him you've got an headache.

Danny He wouldn't finish the work for us though, would he? It's not fair to leave it for night staff. I hate night shift. Keep yer for hours if you don't get stuff done.

Racheal I'd like to see you.

Danny Would you?

Racheal Yeah. Will you ring us?

Danny Yeah. Course.

Racheal Will you?

Danny I told you I would, didn't I?

Racheal You promise?

Danny What's the matter with you, eh?

Racheal I don't know. I just. I just get. I'd just like to see you. There's nothing the matter with me.

Danny Rache.

Racheal What?

Danny I brought you a present.

Racheal Yer what?

Danny This morning. On way in. I got you a present.

Racheal (*not delighted*) Did yer?

Danny It's a bit shit.

Racheal Is it?

Danny I'm bollocks at buying presents, me. I'm shit at it. But. I just wanted to get you something.

Racheal Right.

Danny I never had time to wrap it.

Racheal That's all right.

Danny *passes her a paper bag. From the bag she takes out a small jewellery box. Inside the box there is a gold bracelet. He watches her, anxious.*

Racheal (*doesn't look at him*) It's . . . Danny. This is a bit mad.

Danny Does it fit you?

Racheal (*trying it on*) Course. Look. (*Beat.*) I can't take this.

Danny Course you can –

Racheal Danny –

Danny I just wanted to. Last night, y'know.

Racheal I know.

She looks at him only now. Goes towards him. Goes as though to kiss him. But doesn't.

Thank you. Go back to work now.

Danny I'll ring you when I'm done.

Racheal All right.

Danny We could go Savoy or summit.

Racheal We could do, yes.

Danny   You coming down with us?

Racheal   No. Give us a minute. Gotta sort me timesheets out and that. I'm a bit all over the place.

Danny   Say goodbye to us before you go, won't you?

Racheal   Soft bugger.

Danny   I'll see you later.

Racheal   Yeah. See you in a bit.

He leaves. She watches him go smiling.

She moves into the girls' room and pulls out timesheets from the clipboard. Sits on the bench. Starts filling one out. Clips it back and hangs the clipboard up. Stops. Stares at her bracelet. Takes it off. Stares some more. Hits her head against the locker, gently, five times. Rests her head against it. Whispers 'Danny Danny Danny Danny Danny. You . . .' Stands up straight. Goes to leave. Pauses. Gathers her breath as though screwing up her courage to face something inexorable. Leaves.

Should it be decided not to have an interval here, then the lights should dim and **Racheal** *should change according to the convention that has been established.*

Scene Six

1999. A hotel room. The Fir Tree Hotel, Edale, Derbyshire. New Year's Eve. The last night of the millennium. Pitch black outside. The room is a warm bubble of light around a bed and a dressing table. There is a large mirror. And a small fridge.

Racheal Keats *sits at the dressing table. She wears a short black dress. Her hair is tied up. She is applying make up. She is twenty-one years old.*

Her husband, **Kevin Brake**, *a wiry man, tied up like a knot, stands behind her. He is twenty-eight years old. He wears black jeans*

*and no shoes, socks or shirt. He is drinking from a bottle of Corona. He
is watchful. Slightly drunk.*

Racheal   Funny looking in the mirror and seeing this
room, Kevin.

He looks at her.

Yer get used to seeing rooms in mirrors. When you're doing
your make-up. Your hair and that. When you see a new
room. It looks odd.

He puts on his shirt. Smiles at her.

Been ages since I've stayed in a hotel. Years.

*Puts his shoes and socks on, ties his laces. She drinks from a glass of
wine by her side. Turns to him.*

It's a beautiful part of the world this.

He goes over to the window and stares out.

I love it, all the hills. The smell of the air. You go for walks
round here and you don't see anybody for miles. Only
sheep. Come right up to you. Eat your butties. Find little
pubs. Have a pint. By the fire sometimes. Get a nice packet
of crisps. My mum used to come up here. She told us. When
she were little. Yer can see this place from our dad's flat
sometimes. On a clear day and that. Not this hotel. But
round about here.

*He looks at her for a long time while she continues her make-up.
Finishes his bottle.*

Kevin   You're funny.

Racheal   What?

Kevin   You.

Racheal   What?

Kevin   Nothing.

She drinks some wine. Sprays perfume on to her wrists and applies it to her neck.

Racheal   So. You excited?

Kevin   Excited?

Racheal   About tonight?

Kevin   I am, yeah.

Racheal   Big night, innit?

Kevin   It's the biggest, Racheal.

Racheal   Amazing when you think about it. (*Beat.*) Do you think of it, Kev, as the last night of this millennium or the first night of the next one?

Kevin   I don't know.

Racheal   'Cause when you think about it it could be either, couldn't it?

Kevin   It could be, yeah.

Racheal   I think about it as a beginning. The beginning of something.

Kevin   I hope so.

They smile at each other.

How late's the bar on until.

Racheal   Four o'clock. I think.

Kevin   It better have Jack Daniel's.

Racheal   It will.

Kevin (*patting her back*)   I'm telling you, Rache, it better fucking had do. You go to some of these places, don't you though? Some of these fucking old country places and they don't have anything fucking any good. All fucking bald bastards with brandy and real ale and cigars and wank like that. I'm just drinking Jack Daniel's, me. Tonight. And champagne.

Racheal (*smiling at his description*)   Yer want another tinny?

Kevin   Yeah. Go on.

She goes to fridge. Pulls out another can of Special Brew and the opened bottle of wine. Tops up her glass. Gives him the can. Goes back to the dressing table. Sprays herself with a touch more perfume.

We just got to keep it together.

Racheal   Yer what?

Kevin   Us two.

Racheal   What are you like?

Kevin   That's what matters.

Racheal   Get you.

Kevin   What?

Racheal (*imitating*)   'We just gott akeep it together. That's what matters.'

Kevin   What?

Racheal   Nothing.

Kevin   What, Racheal?

Racheal   Nothing. Honest.

Some time.

Kevin (*honestly, as though gently scared*)   I hate the countryside. It's too quiet.

Racheal   I like that.

Kevin (*the same*)   At night-time. You open your window. You can't hear nothing. Scares the shit out of us.

Racheal   You can hear foxes. Owls and that.

Kevin   And it's so fucking dark. Can't fucking see anything. Yer need, yer need, yer need, yer need. I don't know. Something.

Racheal   I think that's nice. Makes me feel cosy. Safe.

He looks at her for some time.

Kevin   You smell nice.

Racheal   Thank you.

Kevin   Is that a new perfume?

Racheal   It is, yes.

Kevin   It's nice.

Racheal   Billy got it for us.

Kevin   Did he?

Racheal   For Christmas.

Kevin   That's nice.

Some time.

Did he nick it?

Racheal   Kevin!

Kevin   What?

Racheal   No.

Kevin   You sure?

Racheal   He bought it. He's got a job and everything.

Kevin   Has he?

Racheal   He's working in Bull's Head.

Kevin   He all right, is he?

Racheal   He is. Yeah. Been six month now.

Kevin   Good lad. Six month, eh? Fuck me. How's yer old man?

Racheal He's all right. Bit. Yer know.

Kevin What?

Racheal Bit moody.

Kevin Is he?

Racheal Strops about. Like a big kid.

Kevin You nearly finished.

Racheal Just do my hair.

He watches her as she lets her hair down and starts to comb it.

Kevin Tell you one good thing about hotel.

Racheal What's that?

Kevin It's very tidy int it? (*He grins, squeezes his eyes tight. Opens them again and breathes out a sigh of relief.*) Not like our fucking dump. Eh, Racheal?

No response. He coughs once.

Sometimes wonder, honestly, sometimes I wonder what the fuck you actually do all day.

Racheal Yer what? Kevin?

Kevin So, your kid, he still hanging round all Chris Bennett? That lot. Lucy Moore?

Racheal Yeah.

Kevin He see much of Danny Miller?

Racheal Don't know. A bit.

Kevin What do you mean?

Racheal Yer what?

Kevin You said you don't know and then you said 'a bit'. Which is it?

Racheal I think he sees him every so often.

Kevin   Yer know that, do yer?

Racheal   Yeah.

Kevin (*quietly, grinning*)   So, if you know that, if you know that Rache, how come you said you didn't know when I first asked you?

Racheal   You what?

Kevin (*still*)   You heard. Bit fucking weird that, int it?

Racheal   Kev –

Kevin (*louder*)   No it is though, a bit fucking weird. Int it though? It fucking is. Why did you lie to us, Racheal?

Racheal   I wasn't lying, Kevin. I just wasn't thinking. I was just, y'know.

Kevin   No. I don't know, Rache. I don't know at all. What were you just doing? You were just – what?

Racheal   I was talking without really thinking about what I was saying. That's not lying. That's different from lying. Kev, are you all right?

Kevin   Me? I'm fine. Fucking great, yeah. Cracking. Never better. Yer just . . .

Racheal   What?

Kevin   You look lovely, Racheal. You know that. You do, sweetheart.

Racheal   Thank you.

Kevin   You look . . .

Racheal   What?

Kevin   When was the last time you saw him?

Racheal   Who?

Kevin   Danny Miller.

Racheal   Two years ago.

Kevin   Was it?

Racheal   Just before we got married.

Kevin (*looking at her first*)   Are you sure?

Racheal   Yes.

Kevin   You're not just talking without really thinking what you're saying now, are you, Rache?

Racheal   No. Just after I left Somerfield. Down White Lion. I remember it.

Kevin   I bet you do.

Racheal   Yer what?

Kevin   I said I bet you remember seeing him. I fucking bet you do.

Racheal   Kev, please, don't.

Kevin   Don't what?

Racheal   Just . . .

Kevin   Don't what, Racheal? I don't *believe* you. So. Can I ask you a question? Rache? Can I? Rache, look at us. Rache, if your perfume is a Christmas present, Racheal, if your perfume is a Christmas present, how come the bottle's not full?

Racheal   Yer what?

Kevin   It's not though, is it? Look. There's some gone out of that.

Racheal   There's never –

Kevin   Rache, there fucking is. Of course there fucking is. I can see there fucking is just by fucking looking at the cunt.

Racheal   Kev.

Kevin (*picking the bottle up*)   Now. If this was a Christmas present from your brother that you got last Saturday yes?

And this is the first time I have seen you wear it yes? Then how come there is some taken out of the bottle?

Racheal   Kev, I swear –

Kevin   That must mean, Rache, when you think about it and everything, that must mean that either a) your brother gave you a half-full bottle of perfume for your Christmas present, which is a bit fucking mard-arsed of him in my opinion, or b) you've worn it before somewhere else when you went out with someone else, you've worn it for someone else, without letting me know. It must do, Rache, mustn't it?

Racheal   No, Kev –

Kevin   It must do. Really. Come on, Rache. I'm not a fucking thick cunt. Which is it?

Racheal   What?

Kevin   Which is it? Did your skinny-arsed fucking rat of a brother give you some dodgy cheap shitty bottle of half-filled fucking perfume or have you worn it before? This week? When I've been out? Which is it?

Racheal   Kev, neither – it's not half –

Kevin   Which is it?

Racheal   I can't do this.

Kevin   Do what?

Racheal   I haven't got the energy any more, Kevin.

Kevin   Which is it, Racheal?

Racheal   It's not half opened.

Kevin   Racheal, which is it?

Racheal   Kev.

Kevin   Don't you fucking lie to me. I'll break your fucking teeth. Which is it?

Racheal   Kevin, don't.

Kevin Which is it, Racheal?

Racheal It's neither, I swear.

Kevin Why are you lying to me? Racheal? Why?

Racheal I'm not.

Kevin (*perhaps punches his chest with each beat*)   Why? Why?
Why? Why? Why?

*Throws the perfume against the floor. It smashes. He pulls back.
Finishes his can. Stares at her while she talks. Nodding his head.
Chewing frantically.*

Racheal I thought we could have a night out. Just
tonight. Just for the millennium. Just us two. Be nice,
wouldn't it? If just for one night, if just one night. It would
be nice. I hate this. You're just like fucking Dad. Stinks in
here now.

Kevin (*very quietly*)   Where's your phone?

Racheal You what?

Kevin (*still*)   Where's your phone? Racheal? Your mobile
phone.

Racheal What do you want my phone for?

Kevin (*still, he turns to her*)   Where's your fucking phone,
Racheal?

Racheal I'm not telling you. It's my fucking phone.

Kevin (*shouts suddenly*)   Fuck.

Goes to her. Grabs a handful of her hair.

Where's your fucking phone, Racheal.

Racheal Get off me.

Kevin Tell me. Where is it?

Racheal It's in me bag.

He lets her go. She falls to the floor.

That hurt me. You little fuck wad.

Flashes a glare at her. Raises his fist suddenly. She cowers back. He goes over to her bag. Pulls the stuff out of her bag randomly, wantonly, throwing it around. Pulls her phone out. Finds her phone-book function on it. Lists through the names kept on the phone.

Kevin   Where are we? Where are we? Come on? Where are we?

Racheal   What are you doing?

Kevin   C, C, C, C, C – d. Danny. Fuck. You lying fucking cunt.

Racheal   Kev, I swear.

Kevin   Who's Danny, Racheal? Heh? Who's that? Fucking Danny? Who's fucking Danny, Racheal? Is it Danny Miller? Is it?

Racheal   Kev, please, don't.

Kevin   You fucking slag.

Gets her by her hair. Lifts her up. Throws her across the bed. Presses dial on the phone.

It's engaged. It's fucking engaged. C'mon, Danny. You fucking cheap cunt fucker.

Dials redial. It is still engaged.

Fuck. Fuck. Fuck. Fuck. Fuck.

*He smashes his head into the mirror. Three times. It cracks around him. He slumps down on to the floor. Starts sobbing. Huge big sobs. Wails as he inhales. His shoulders heave. **Racheal** doesn't move. Stares at him.*

Kevin (*tiny broken-hearted voice*)   You're my wife. You're supposed to be my wife. See, you know what your problem is? Don't you? You're a fucking tart. Is your problem.

Racheal (*simply*)   I'm not.

Kevin   Just a slapper. Just a slag. Worst day of my life day
I married you. Hated it. Had to get drunk just to get
through it. Manky old slag.

Racheal (*again, simply*)   I'm not, Kev. Don't say that.

Kevin   Don't you fucking dare even think about telling me
what to do.

He stares at her for a while. And then stands.

I'm going out now. I don't know when I'm coming back. I
hope you die soon.

He leaves. She watches him go.

*Stands up after a while. It hurts. She goes to pick up her wine glass.
Drains it. Gets the wine bottle from the fridge and refills her glass. She
goes to where* **Kevin** *has dropped her phone and picks it up. Sits back
on the bed. Drinks from her glass. Phones her brother.*

Racheal   Billy? Billy? Hello, love. It's me, Racheal. How
are you? Are you? Good. Good lad. Are you? That'll be
good, won't it? I'm OK. I'm OK, love. I'm fine. I'm good.
Yeah. Just. I don't know. I don't think so. No. Kevin's had a
bit of a bad one, mate, you with me? No. No I'm fine. He's
just. I hate him, Billy. I want to kill him. I think I might. I
could. I fucking could. I bet you. No. No I won't. No, don't
worry about that. I'll be fine. I will. I'll be, I'll be magic. I
just wanted to talk to you. See how you were getting on. I
was thinking about yer. Got yer perfume on. I have. I have
and all. I like it. It's really nice. Oh, fuck him. I think it's
lovely. I just wanted to wish you Happy New Year. I know
well. I'm doing it early, aren't I? Happy New Year. I know.
Happy New Century. Happy New Millennium. It's mental,
int it? Listen, mate, I'm gonna fuck off. I'll not keep you. I
just wanted to, you know, I just wanted to talk to you.
Good. Good. Good. No. I'll be, I'm fine. I'm cracking.
Yeah. You have a good night, mate. Yeah. I know. I love
you, Bill. Well. I do. I'll see you later. Have a good one.
Have a good night. See you later.

She turns the phone off. Sits up on the bed. Staring out of the window.

Stands up after a while.

The lights fade. She walks right to the very edge of the stage. Puts on a small black cardigan.

Scene Seven

2002. The beer garden at the front of the Elizabethan Pub, Heaton Moor, Stockport.

It is ten o'clock at night. Towards the end of summer. The first night when you notice that the temperature has begun to drop.

There is a wooden table in the centre of the stage. Two wooden benches are attached, one either side.

Racheal Keats, *twenty-four, enters. She has just walked out of the pub. Something about her demeanour, the way she holds herself, the way she glances back to where she came from suggests that something has happened inside the pub to upset her. She stands in the middle of the stage. As though on the cusp of leaving the beer garden. But stops herself. Wraps her arms around herself to keep her warm.*

After a short while, **Danny Miller**, *also aged twenty-four, in a short-sleeved shirt and jeans comes out to find her. He carries her vodka and lime, half drunk, and his half-drunk pint of lager. He expects her to have left the beer garden. When he realises she hasn't he pulls himself up short.*

She becomes aware of his presence. Straightens. Doesn't look back at him.

Danny (*tentative*)   So. Did you miss us?

Racheal (*still not looking back, not smiling*)   Course.

Danny   Should have rung us. We could have come to see you.

Racheal (*still not*)   I know. I'm sorry.

Danny   Always wanted to go to York.

Racheal (*still not*)   It's very pretty.

Danny   Go t'races. Check out minster. All that.

Racheal   Good pubs and all.

Danny   Are there?

Racheal   Cracking, aye.

Danny   Are you all right?

Racheal   Yeah. Funny.

Danny   What?

Racheal (*with a nod back to the pub*)   In there. All them cunts. Look at yer. Like. Once you've left you can't ever go back. Who do they think they are?

Danny   I don't know.

She turns back to him.

How long were you there for?

Racheal   Ten month. Bit more.

Danny *pulls out a cigarette. Lights it, looking at her.*

Danny   Did you enjoy yourself, Racheal?

Racheal   Yeah. I did. It was all right.

Danny   Is it very different?

Racheal   What?

Danny (*putting the drinks down next to her*)   York. From Stockport?

Racheal   I don't know. It feels smaller. It's older. With the wall and that. Load of fucking students. Shops are all right.

Danny   Did you . . . ?

Racheal   What?

Danny   I don't know.

Racheal *smiles. Moves towards him.*

Danny (*puts drinks on table*)   You make any friends there?

Racheal   Couple. They were all right. Couple of girls from work. People were well friendly, mind you. Go into pubs and folk just talk to you.

Danny   What about fellas?

Racheal (*turns to face him briefly, with a smile*)   What about fellas?

Danny   Meet anybody?

Racheal   No one special. Not really. Couple of morons.

Danny   York City casuals?

Racheal   Yeah, right.

Danny   You not cold?

Racheal   No I'm fine.

Danny   What's it like coming back?

Racheal   It's all right.

Danny   Notice anything different?

Racheal (*grins before she speaks*)   You've had your hair cut.

Danny   No. About Stockport.

Racheal   Only weird stuff.

Danny   What like?

Racheal   I noticed how short the clock tower in Merseyway was.

Danny   You what?

Racheal (*walks once around the table*)   When I was a kid I used to think it was massive. Fucking big skyscraper. I couldn't understand how come, when they had programmes about the tallest buildings in the world, I couldn't understand why they never mentioned the clock tower in Merseyway. I went back in there at the weekend. It's tiny. Very squat. Really short. I was quite disappointed. Noticed the viaduct.

Danny   The viaduct?

Racheal   I never really paid any attention to it before. I never really noticed it. But I was looking at it, on my way into town. It's actually, y'know, it's quite impressive. There's something about it.

Danny   Single largest brick structure in the world.

Racheal   Oh aye?

Danny   It is actually.

Racheal   I noticed how many pubs there are. Pubs fucking everywhere in this place. A lot of the shops have changed. Smartened up a bit.

Danny   Still fucking grotty, mind you.

Racheal   I don't know. Some of them are all right. And I was up at the station. Looking down. Noticed the way the valley curves down.

Danny   Oh aye?

Racheal   When I was little, I used to love all geography. All about continental drift. And the ice age. Stuff like that. And looking at the town centre I could just have imagined what it must have been like. All the ice and that. How it would have settled. See all the curves of where the water was. Imagine what it was like underneath the sea. That was a bit mad.

Danny   Sounds it.

She is on the point of sitting at the table. But then doesn't. Takes a drink. Moves away again. Folds her arms again. He settles on the bench.

Racheal   Funny going back into Manchester. All the rain.
Went in with Billy. It were pissing down. Felt, kind of, it felt
all right. Felt like it was meant to be raining here. Felt OK.
You know what I mean?

Danny   Built on rain. Manchester. All towns round here.

Racheal   Yer what?

Danny (*follows her*)   Whole city only settled where it is
because the air was so moist. Made it all right for cotton
industry. All factories and that. If it hadn't rained so much it
wouldn't have even been here.

Racheal   Is that right?

Danny   Fucking dead right.

Racheal   Yer know a lot of funny stuff, you, don't you?

Danny   It's not funny. It's good.

Racheal   I did miss you. Funny that, int it? Mind you.
You little bugger. Yer could have rang us.

Danny   I couldn't find you.

Racheal   Could have told us.

Danny   Didn't know where you were.

Racheal   Could have asked our kid.

Danny   He was –

Racheal   Well, our dad then.

Danny   I . . .

Racheal (*moves away from him*)   Could have tried. I would
have loved to have come. I'd love to meet her, Sarah.

Danny (*stays where he is*)   You'd like her.

Racheal   You reckon?

Danny   She's very, I don't know, she's, she's tough. Is what she is. She's not thick. You know? Don't take shit from anybody. I, I, I really, yer know, I love her and that.

Racheal   I should hope so.

Danny   I do.

Racheal (*turns to face him*)   How old's Hazel?

Danny   She's two next September.

Racheal   Good age that, int it?

Danny   She's funny.

Racheal   With all the talking and that?

Danny   Yer should hear her.

Racheal   I can imagine. Would y'ave another one?

Danny   Maybe. One day. I hope so.

Racheal   I bet yer a great dad, you.

Danny   I don't know about that.

Racheal   I bet you are. I bet she loves you like mad.

Danny (*drinks*)   I wish I didn't have to work so much. So I could spend more time with her. All that.

Racheal   How is your work?

Danny   It's all right. Nice and quiet this time of year. Everybody's fucked off on holiday. Gets a bit mad around Christmas. All cards and that.

Racheal   You got a uniform?

Danny   Course.

Racheal   I bet you look dead cute in it.

Danny   Fuck off.

Racheal   Like yer dressing up or summit.

Danny   Sometimes think I'll jack it in.

Racheal   Why?

Danny   Sort something out. Set something up. Work for myself or summit. Sometimes I think I'd like to do that.

Racheal   Doing what?

While he talks he taps his fag packet.

Danny   Mate of mine's got a little company. Does panelling. Yer know, for people's houses. Pubs and that. Couple of months back he was having a bit of a rush on. Asked us if I could help him out. It were magic.

He takes a cigarette out.

Racheal   Was it?

He points with his cigarette to punctuate his observations.

Danny   It was quite, you know, it was creative. Yer had to think and that. But then after a bit, you get into it, get a rhythm going. And when you look at it all done. It looks quite, like, quite beautiful. You just, you just ended up thinking just – well, well, what the fuck?

Lights cigarette.

Racheal   Be great.

Danny   Get a little van. Pop Hazel up in the passenger seat. Whizz all round. Doing panels. I'd love that. I think about it quite a lot.

Racheal   You should do it.

Danny   Yeah. Maybe.

Beat.

He looks down at his cigarette. Smokes from it. Embarrassed by giving himself away a little. **Racheal** *smiles at him.*

Rache.

Racheal Yeah.

Danny I was sorry to hear about Kevin.

Racheal (*turning away*) Oh yeah.

Danny He sounds like he was a fucking cunt.

Racheal He was.

Danny Yer seen him? Since you've come back?

Racheal Fuck off.

Danny Good. I'm glad. I don't think you should either. He don't deserve you.

Racheal No. He don't.

Danny I couldn't believe it. When I heard what he'd done.

Racheal (*turning back*) It was just a big. Horrible. Mistake. I should never have even. I don't know what I was thinking about. Just with, just with, with Lucy and Chris and everybody seemed to be, and he was there. And he was quite, yer know, he still is, quite handsome. He asks us. I just think well, Rache, yer may as well. It's convenient.

Looks straight at him.

How shit is that?

Danny I know.

Racheal Convenient. I hope you never do anything like that because it's convenient, Danny. I really hope you don't, love.

Beat.

She looks away only briefly. Goes to the table again. Stands by it, resting her weight on her knee against it.

You see much of Chris and Lucy?

Danny   Yeah. From time to time. You should give 'em a ring.

Racheal   I will.

Danny   Go out with Chris every so often. Have a bevvy.

Racheal   They happy?

Danny   Lucy's expecting.

Racheal   Is she?

Danny   Next February.

Racheal   Fucking hell. Are they excited?

Danny   Yeah. She is. She'll be great. Comes round to play with Hazel every now and then. Hazel loves her. I think Chris is a bit freaked out.

Racheal   Bless him.

Danny   Yer get like that. Most blokes. I think. And then when the baby's born. It's just, it's different. It changes. They live up in Offie.

Racheal   Do they?

Danny   Top of Dialstone Road.

Racheal   Oh aye.

Danny   Back behind of Elm's House.

Racheal   Ha!

She pushes herself away from the table again.

Danny   What?

Racheal   That's where our gran lived.

Danny   Is it?

Racheal   Yeah. She died last year. (*Beat.*) Weird.

Danny   What?

Racheal   How small things are.

Danny   Yeah.

Beat. He moves towards her slightly.

How's your dad?

Racheal   He's all right. Bit drunk. Can be a bit of a fuckhead.

Danny   You staying with him?

Racheal   For the time being. It's all right. I don't see much of him. He sleeps quite a lot of the time.

Danny   If you ever want a break, y'know, Rache? We've got a spare room and that. Could come and crash with us.

Racheal   Thanks. I'll be all right. He's changed.

Danny   Has he?

Racheal   He seems much more gentle.

Danny   Right. That's good.

Racheal   In the morning and that he brings us a cup of tea in bed, if he's up.

Danny   Well, we wouldn't do that for yer. That's certainly fucking true. (*He moves closer.*) How's your Billy?

Racheal   He's Billy. Yer know. Not been run over for a long time.

Danny   Yer what?

Racheal   Do yer not remember? He were always getting, every week, for a while, he couldn't move without being hit by a bloody car.

Danny   I don't remember.

Racheal   It was never serious. Years ago now.

Danny   When did he get out?

Racheal   February.

Danny   Is he getting any help or anything?

Racheal   Bits. He goes to see probation. He's trying to sort himself out with another job. It's not easy.

Danny   No.

She moves away from him.

Racheal (*talking out*)   But he's done well. Yer hear stories of people who go down. Getting all fucked up with all kinds of stuff. He don't. He don't do drugs. Nowt like that. He just. He really tries. I hope . . . (*Turns back.*) This is a very big chance for him. I hope he doesn't fuck things up this time. I hope he'll be all right.

Danny   I'm sure he will.

Racheal   You should go and see him. He'd love to, you know. He always really liked you.

Danny   Did he?

Racheal   He looked up to you.

Danny   Fucking hell.

Racheal   You know he did.

Beat.

She looks at **Danny** *before she speaks to him.*

Danny.

Danny   Yeah.

Racheal   Yer know you said you loved Sarah?

Danny   Yeah.

Racheal   Would you say you were in love with her as well?

Danny   I think so. Yeah. I would.

Racheal   That's good.

Danny   Yeah. I think it is.

Racheal   What do you think the difference is?

Danny   I don't know.

Racheal   Do you know what I think the difference is?

Danny   Go on.

Racheal   I think if you're in love with somebody then what you've got is a pure compatibility. There's something, it's just, it's pure. Is what it is. I think there's something pure about it.

Danny   Maybe.

Racheal   Just pure. (*Beat.*) I've never had that. Not with anybody. Never. You know what the closest I ever came was?

Danny   What?

Racheal   When I was with you. I thought . . . We did all right, didn't we? And you know what? You know what I was thinking, what I was going to. Actually. You know what I was going to ask you? You know what I was going to ask? Do you think, did you ever think, if I asked you to leave Sarah, and leave Hazel, and come and live somewhere with me, you'd say no, wouldn't you?

Long pause. The two don't shake eye contact from one another.

Danny (*very quietly*)   Yes. I would.

Racheal   I knew you would.

Danny   I'm sorry.

Racheal (*looking away from him*)   No. Don't be. Don't be sorry, Danny. Honestly. It was just something I was thinking. (*Looks back to him again.*) I think about you all the time.

Danny   I know.

Racheal   Sometimes I just sit down and I just think why the fuck did I do that?

Danny   I know.

Racheal   I, I, I . . .

Danny   It's hard. Int it?

She looks at him. And then turns away and can't look back.

After a pause.

Racheal   I keep having these nightmares.

Danny   Nightmares?

Racheal   Stupid ones. About our grandad. And our nana. About all these folk. Fucking Paul Castle's brother. Sarah Briard.

Danny   Who?

Racheal   Just this girl from our primary school. She died when I was ten. She wanted to play for Man U. I keep dreaming about people I know and who have died. It does my head in. Dream they're in the house with us. Watching us.

Long pause.

Danny   Yer know what I think?

Racheal   What?

Danny   What I think about ghosts?

Racheal   What?

Danny   I don't think they exist, Racheal.

Racheal (*turns to him and then away*)   Don't you?

Danny   I think you need to go somewhere.

Racheal   Yer what?

Danny   Somewhere, maybe, maybe, maybe somewhere you used to go with yer grandad or your brother or your mum –

Racheal   My mum?

Danny   Or summit. And just spend a night there. Watch the morning come up.

Racheal   What the fuck are you going on about, you, eh?

Danny   It's just something I think. It might help. I don't know. (*Pause.*) Rache. (*Pause.*) Rache, look at us. (*Pause.*) Yer know when yer have a mental image of somebody. When you close your eyes and think of somebody just off the top of your head. When I do that and think of you, yer know what I see? (*No response.*) I see you in the morning, on the first morning I stayed over at your house. Waking up. Watching you lying asleep next to me. You looked, you looked. It was like. I think about that more than you probably think I do. (*Pause.*) Rache, I'm really sorry. I can't. I just can't.

Racheal   I know. All right? I know.

She dries her eyes. Looks back at him.

Danny   You all right?

She laughs once. Gently. Smiles at him for a moment.

What? What are you smiling about?

Racheal   You.

Danny   What about me?

Racheal   It's just, it's good to see you. I'm glad you're doing all right. Yer know?

Danny   Yes. I do.

Beat. She walks over to him at the table.

You know you'll be all right, mate, don't you?

Racheal   Everybody keeps fucking saying that.

Danny   You will. You'll be, you'll be fucking great, Rache. I swear.

She touches his face with her hand. Lets it fall. Holds his hand. Squeezes it.

Lights dim.

Racheal *goes back to sit in the car.* **Danny** *exits.* **Billy** *joins* **Racheal***.*

Scene Eight

2002. A parked Vauxhall Cavalier in the car park of the flats on Lancashire Hill in Stockport. We should see the interior of the car stripped bare towards the edge of the stage.
   Isolating light on the car.
   Racheal Keats*, aged twenty-four, and* **Billy Keats***, nineteen, stare out looking up at the flats and around the hill into the town.*
   It is four o'clock in the morning.
   Racheal *is in the driver's seat.* **Billy** *in the passenger seat. He tries to lower it as far back as it will go. Tries to sleep. Can't. Raises it back up again. Lights a cigarette.*

Racheal   Shouldn't smoke. Knacker your lungs. Make you sterile. Give you cancer.

Billy *stares at her in utter disbelief.*

Racheal   'S true.

Billy (*about her audacity rather than her science*)   I don't believe you.

Racheal   Well, it is.

Billy   Do you know what time it is?

Racheal   Yeah.

Billy   Well then.

Racheal   What?

Billy   This is stupid.

Racheal   Yer don't have to stay here. I'll be all right on my own.

Billy   Racheal.

Racheal   I'm not a little baby, Bill.

Billy   I'm not leaving you sat out here on yer tod. You said you wanted me to come with you.

Racheal   I do.

Billy   Well, I'm here.

Racheal   Well, open the window.

He does. Yawns. Stretches. Flicks fag ash out of the window. Turns to her.

Billy   What were it you wanted to ask us?

Racheal   You what?

Billy   Before. Said you had summit to ask us. What were it?

Racheal   It can wait.

Billy   I'm knackered, me. Honestly. I'm fucked.

Long pause. Big, big, big yawn from **Billy**. *His movements become agitated. Perhaps he starts tapping his feet under his chair. Drumming on his knees.*

Racheal   Billy.

Billy   Racheal.

Racheal   Do you remember when we came here with Mum? When Dad locked us out?

Billy   Yeah.

Racheal   Do you remember that?

Billy   Course I do.

Racheal   Mad that, weren't it?

Billy   She thumped us.

Racheal   I know. I remember.

Pause.

I knew then that she was gonna go. Y'know? I figured it out.

Pause.

I never told anybody that. You're the first person. Keep your feet still. Always fucking drumming. Like your wired up to the mains or summit.

Beat. He does.

Not changed that much really, has it?

Billy   No.

Racheal   Used to like it here. It were all right. Me and Leanne Macyntyre. Come down here. Look for Ronald Abbey. Smoke fags. Play near the river. Look at the motorway. Throw stones at it.

Billy   That's fucking dangerous. Yer can get sent down for that. I'm telling.

Racheal   Don't.

Billy (*opens his car door, sits sideways, stretching his legs*) Fucking am.

Racheal   Wonder whatever happened to Leanne Macyntyre.

Billy (*lighting another cigarette*)   She fucked off.

Racheal   Did she?

Billy   Ages back. Her and her mum. Went up Sheffield, I think. You remember her mum? I used to fancy her summit rotten.

Racheal   Fucking hell.

Billy   What?

Racheal   Just . . . I wonder what she's doing. Right now. Right this second.

Billy   Probably fucking sleeping I expect. In a fucking bed.

Racheal   Wonder what Ronald Abbey's doing?

Billy   Having a fucking wank knowing him. Thinking about you and Leanne Macyntyre. Happiest days of his life they were. Never been the same since.

Racheal   Sometimes I get quite sad.

Billy   You what?

Racheal   Thinking about people like Leanne Macyntyre. Ronald Abbey.

Billy   What the fuck are you going on about, Rache?

Racheal   Thinking about what they're doing. Dad.

Billy   Yer live with Dad. You fucking live in the room next door to him.

Racheal   Chris and Lucy. Danny. Kevin. Mum. That's the worst one. I get scared about people who've died. And sad about people who I don't really see much any more.

Billy   You're fucking weird.

Racheal   But I'm not sad just now.

Billy   Thank fuck for that.

Racheal   I'm all right. Just, y'know, thinking. (*Beat.*) I saw Danny last week.

Billy   Did ya?

Racheal He told me to say hello to you.

Billy Right. Hello, Danny. How's he doing?

Racheal He's doing all right. He's doing great. Got married. Got a little girl. Hazel. She's two.

Billy That's good, int it? I always used to like him. He was all right.

Racheal Yeah. He was.

Billy Bit chicken, like. But he was all right. (*Beat.*) Yer know what I think's mental.

Racheal What?

Billy (*gesturing out*) Thinking about all t'athletes. Down Manchester.

Racheal Yer what?

Billy All gathered together, like, in one place. Getting ready to compete. I think that's a bit mad. Can y'imagine?

Racheal What?

Billy Being them.

Racheal Yer what?

Billy Being an athlete. Fucking off all over the world. Running and jumping. Being the best in the world and going all over the place doing your stuff. That'd be mental, wouldn't it?

Racheal Yeah.

Billy It would though, wouldn't it, Rache? I'd love that. I used to be a right cracking little runner me.

Racheal Shoulda stuck at it.

Billy Shoulda done.

Climbs back in the car. Lowers his seat slightly. Leans back.

Racheal Billy.

Billy Rache.

Racheal What are you gonna do?

Billy You what?

Racheal What are you gonna do? It's been five month now.

Billy I know. Is this what you wanted to ask us about?

Racheal Yer not . . .

Billy What?

Racheal Yer not gonna start nicking stuff again, are you?

Billy Is this what you wanted to ask us about, Rache?

Racheal Not only this. You're not though, are you?

Billy No. No way, mate.

Racheal I really don't want you to go back down.

Billy Yer fucking telling me.

Racheal I worry about you.

Billy Do you?

Racheal Because I know it's difficult. Getting a job and that.

Billy Difficult int the fucking word, Rache, you with me?

Racheal Billy, what was it like?

Billy What was what like?

Racheal Inside.

Billy It was horrible.

Racheal Why?

Billy Just . . .

Racheal What was horrible about it, Billy?

Billy   I don't really want to talk about this Racheal.

Racheal   Was it different to young offenders'?

Billy   Yes.

Racheal   How?

Billy   Look, Rache, I told you. . . Can we just fucking drop it?

Racheal   You should talk about it.

Billy *rolls over in the car seat, away from* **Racheal**. *Covers his head with his coat.*

Billy   Fucking hell.

Racheal   It might help.

Billy   Fuck's sake.

Racheal   Sorry. (*Pause.*) I worry about yer.

Billy   Yer said. Don't bother.

Racheal   It's cause I like yer.

Pause. He looks at her very briefly, still lying down. Uncovers his head.

Billy   It was nasty. (*Pause.*) Does your head in. Gets me thinking odd stuff.

Racheal   What like? What like, Billy? What kind of stuff do yer think about?

Long pause.

Billy   Y'know, at times I imagine myself getting fucking smacked up something rotten or summit.

Racheal   Like what?

Billy   Like heading a flying concrete football. Getting smacked in the face by a metal girder. Having an iron spike cutting right through my brain. Yer know what I mean?

Racheal   I'm not sure.

Billy   I think about that stuff when I think about going down.

Racheal   I see.

Long pause. **Billy** *props himself up. Looks out of the window.*

Billy   Do you know how old the world is?

Racheal   No.

Billy   Five hundred million years old. They reckon.

Racheal   How do you know that?

Billy   I read it. In nick. And scientists are starting to think that it might be even older.

Racheal   Are they?

Billy   Do you know how long human beings have been around on it?

Racheal   How long?

Billy   Fifty thousand years. It's fucking nothing. We don't matter a jot. Not one jot.

Racheal   I don't think that's true.

Billy   It fucking is.

Racheal   Did you cry ever?

Billy   Yer what?

Racheal   When you were in prison did you used to cry? (*No response.*) What's your favourite colour?

Billy   I'm not playing this.

Racheal   Go on.

Billy   No. I'm too tired. I'm all –

Racheal   Yer know what I reckon?

Billy   What?

Racheal   You know what I think. I think that nobody or nothing should make you cry. Ever. And I'm sorry because I know that there are some things that I just don't know about prison and about what it was like and what happened and all that. But I do get you now. I do get you. And I didn't always but I do now. And I love yer. And I do think that you will be all right.

Billy   You don't know what you're talking about.

Racheal   You know I said that there was something I was going to ask you.

Billy   Yeah.

Racheal   Billy, I think I might go away again.

Billy   Right.

Racheal   But for a long time this time. Not just a few months. For years. And maybe, go, maybe even leave the country even. Go and live somewhere else completely. I wanted to talk to you about it. I wanted to know what you thought about it.

Billy   What I thought about it? What's it got to do with me?

Racheal   I wanted to check that you'd be all right. If I went away.

Billy   If I'd be all right?

Racheal   I'm still not sure. I still, I haven't really decided if I should go now or if I should go at all of if I should –

Billy   I think you should. I think you should go. I think you should go now. I think you should just fuck off.

Racheal   Yer what?

Billy   I think you should.

Racheal   Right.

Billy   I mean people should. You know? It's not enough to just stay somewhere. You can't do, all your life, you can't do things just for me. Or for Dad. Or any of that. It'd fucking kill your head, mate, you with me?

Racheal   I am. Yeah.

Billy   This place is just, it's odd. You should go and look at stuff. You might come back, mightn't you?

Racheal   I might do. Yeah.

Pause. He looks at her. She looks up at the flat.

I want to go to college.

Billy   That's a top idea.

Racheal   Go and get trained up. Get some qualifications.

Billy   Qualifications?

Racheal   I want to work as a nursery nurse. Do it properly. Get certificates and that.

Billy   You'd be very good at that.

Racheal   And I really want to get a dog.

Billy   A dog?

Racheal   I couldn't get a dog in the flats and Stockport isn't a very good place for a dog anyway.

Billy   What are you talking about? Loads of people have dogs in Stockport. Fucking hundreds. Anyway. Dogs stink.

Racheal   They don't.

Billy   They fucking do. (*Beat.*) I hope it works.

Racheal   What?

Billy   This. (*Beat.*) Or going away. Or whatever.

Long pause. The two of them look out.

I think about Mum all the time.

Racheal   So do I.

Billy   I hope she's all right.

Racheal   So do I.

Billy   She broke my heart though.

Racheal   Mine and all.

Billy   I'm going to go to sleep now.

Racheal   All right.

Billy   If I can get fucking comfy.

Racheal   Good luck.

Billy   G'night.

Racheal   Good night.

Long pause.

Sun's coming up.

Billy   Yer what?

Racheal   Look. Up over hills. Sun's coming up.

She points out of car window. He moves his head to look but doesn't move out of his reclined position. Settles his head back down. She looks straight ahead for a while.

Blackout.

Printed in the USA
CPSIA information can be obtained
at www.ICGtesting.com
LVHW041059171024
794057LV00001B/164

9 780413 773111